Reality

For Alanna, John, and Doug

Reality TV

June Deery

polity

Copyright © June Deery 2015

The right of June Deery to be identified as Author of this Work has been asserted in accordance with the UK Copyright, Designs and Patents Act 1988.

First published in 2015 by Polity Press

Polity Press
65 Bridge Street
Cambridge CB2 1UR, UK

Polity Press
350 Main Street
Malden, MA 02148, USA

ISBN-13: 978-0-7456-5242-9
ISBN-13: 978-0-7456-5243-6(pb)

A catalogue record for this book is available from the British Library.

Library of Congress Cataloging-in-Publication Data

Deery, June.
  Reality TV / June Deery.
    pages cm
  Includes bibliographical references and index.
  ISBN 978-0-7456-5242-9 (hardback : alk. paper) -- ISBN 978-0-7456-5243-6 (pbk. : alk. paper) 1. Reality television programs--History and criticism. I. Title.
  PN1992.8.R43D44 2015
  791.45'309--dc23
          2014035165

Typeset in 11/13 Sabon by
Servis Filmsetting Limited, Stockport, Cheshire
Printed and bound in the United Kingdom by CPI Group (UK) Ltd, Croydon CR0 4YY

The publisher has used its best endeavours to ensure that the URLs for external websites referred to in this book are correct and active at the time of going to press. However, the publisher has no responsibility for the websites and can make no guarantee that a site will remain live or that the content is or will remain appropriate.

Every effort has been made to trace all copyright holders, but if any have been inadvertently overlooked the publisher will be pleased to include any necessary credits in any subsequent reprint or edition.

For further information on Polity, visit our website:
politybooks.com

Contents

Acknowledgments

I am very grateful to friends and colleagues at Rensselaer who in the last few years have offered encouragement and advice: especially Ellen Esrock, Katya Haskins, Jim Zappen, Pat Search, and Debbie Kaminski. Thanks also to Patricia Murphy for keeping me in touch with the British scene, as well as our past. A sabbatical enabled me to get this project off the ground and I wish to acknowledge this gift of time and support from Dean Mary Simoni and RPI.

My thanks go to Laurie Ouellette, Misha Kavka, James Hay, Vicki Mayer, and John Corner for their inspiration, encouragement, and correspondence regarding reality TV and to Brenda Weber for organizing a stimulating conference devoted to the subject. I am grateful to Britney Summit-Gil and Jackie Bowler for feedback on the introduction and to Mark Maiellaro and Xander Cesari for their technical help. I also wish to thank the anonymous reviewers who helped me improve the manuscript and the understanding editorial staff at Polity, especially Andrea Drugan, Elen Griffiths and Ian Tuttle. It was a pleasure working with you and I appreciate your being so decent about word limits and deadlines. To Heather, Paul, and everyone at Ellis Oncology Radiology, my thanks for being extraordinarily kind and upbeat during a difficult time. Thanks also to my extended family in Northern Ireland for their good wishes and good craic.

Final thanks I owe to Alanna and John for tolerating people who write books and to Doug who has witnessed another difficult birth.

Also thanks, John, for all the fish.

1

Introduction: Definitions, History, Critiques

I'm not here to make friends. The tribe has spoken. You're fired! I believe in being honest. She has no class. He's not being real. She just threw me under the bus. Move that bus! I can't believe it's me/my living room/my car. I've learned a lot about myself. She is not here for the right reasons. Will you accept this rose? I did it for the experience. I have a friend who's an expert. Make it work. It's my day! Is this your dress? Watch out bitches! This isn't the last you'll hear from me . . .

These catchphrases are heard day after day on screens around the world. Many would recognize them as the voices of reality TV, a type of programming that whether enjoyed or criticized or both has affected television in each of the areas of production, distribution and consumption. So how did this happen and why is it important?

Reality TV is important in the most basic terms because it pervades TV schedules around the world and has, as a consequence, entered all kinds of popular and elite discourse, from personal blogs to presidential politics.[1] To dismiss reality TV because of its often trivial content would be to miss its significance. Some individual programs are of high quality, are well-conceived, or are provocative in important ways; most, on the other hand, are not. Nevertheless, it is impact, tenacity, and cultural resonance, not profundity of content, that make reality television worth analyzing. Even if it were to disappear tomorrow, it would be worth knowing why it arose and was so popular. But for so prominent a cultural form, reality TV is not often or easily defined. *What* is

1

it, and just as interestingly *why* is it, are questions worth asking. In this study, I offer an overview for those who are looking for a broad assessment of where we are with this attention-grabbing phenomenon. Based on current critical scholarship, I have selected what I believe are the main topics and questions reality TV (RTV) poses for students of the media and of contemporary culture.

Among academics, reality TV is becoming one of the most thoroughly analyzed areas of media production. It brings to the fore issues such as: What is real or fictional, how can we recognize either, and is it disturbing if we can't? What does it mean to represent the self and what self are we encouraged to represent? How does watching ordinary people on TV relate to surveillance and governance? Is everything in contemporary culture commodifiable? Is the private still a meaningful designation? Is celebrity ordinary? And what is the role of television in a digital, mobile environment? This programming allows us to think about a cluster of contemporary concerns, including the requirement that we all perform – because of surveillance, because of the marketization of everyday life, because of the demand for individual impression management. Reality TV has become emblematic of a contemporary monitoring and commercialization of performed and mediated identities. It grew in a time of transparency, with people posting intimate information about themselves on social media and conducting loud phone conversations in public. But this is also a time when many are spooked at the discovery of governmental and commercial surveillance. People are giving away privacy but are disturbed when it is not their choice. RTV works through some of these tensions and betrayals.

The nature and novelty of reality TV content also invites fundamental questions about genre, production methods, and motive. Few professional commentators make claims about reality shows being "quality TV," but their popularity and durability have earned them attention and even grudging respect as something deserving analysis. Some reality formats such as the *Big Brother* and *Idol* franchises are the most successful in television history and are significant both for their national and global reach. In many instances, reality TV producers have changed the nature of television and a generation of viewers is growing up that regards unscripted TV as the norm. There are so many reality shows on American and British schedules alone that they are difficult to count: whole channels are devoted to reality programming or are dominated by it.[2] Then, too, a show's impact often extends beyond those who view it and is widely referenced even by people who would bristle at the suggestion that they ever watched it. It is likely that people underreport or underestimate how much reality TV they watch because they don't recognize that what they watch is considered reality TV or, also likely, they underreport because of social stigma – for nothing is easier to criticize in polite society than reality TV. This consensus, too, is noteworthy.

Certainly category identification is not an insignificant problem. "Reality TV" has emerged as a catchall phrase used to describe a wide range of programming but it is to some extent a floating signifier possessing different meanings for different people in different historical moments. One somewhat glib definition of reality TV that I enjoy is "non-fiction television of which I personally disapprove" (Poniewozik 2012: ix). However, I will be using as a basis for discussion the following more specific parameters: *pre-planned but mostly unscripted programming with non-professional actors in non-fictional scenarios*. This is very close to Misha Kavka's initial description of "unscripted shows with non-professional actors being observed by cameras in preconfigured environments" (2012: 5). But as she, too, recognizes, one can soon think of exceptions; for example, the environments aren't always preconfigured, there are different degrees of scripting, and there is even some use of professional actors or certainly aspiring actors. These factors will be examined in more detail later when I propose that reality programming is best defined not according to topic but according to the *relations between the camera, the participants, and the viewers*. For now, I consider the label reality TV useful even when it does not entail precise or agreed on borders. What is included within this category will depend upon which shows are selected as core examples: other programs will have varying strengths of membership. The most reasonable approach is to acknowledge that "reality television" overlaps with

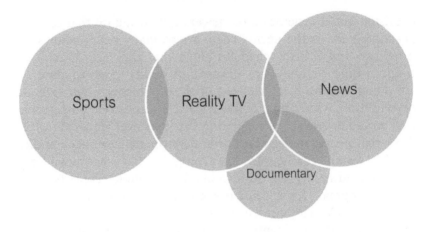

Figure 1 Overlap between reality TV and prior genres

other categories of programming and itself contains distinct but overlapping sub-categories that nevertheless share some common characteristics.

Without engaging in extended comparisons, we can see that reality TV bears some resemblances to prior genres (Fig. 1.1). A large and commercially vital block on most TV schedules is sports programming and this is similar to RTV in that it films actual events ("scripted" only by rules and rituals) and, like some RTV, entertains through the drama of suspenseful competition. Like reality TV also, sports events often happen at all or become important because they will be televised and this mediation shapes content. However, sports broadcasts are typically live (with some limited pre-planned content such as statistical information) and they focus on skills and action more than personalities and interpersonal drama. There is little attention to the emotions or opinions of players who are cast not for their telegenic appearance or acting ambitions but for their athletic performance. The focus is on the extraordinary, but in the sense of being excellent rather than freakish or shameful.

Reality TV also shares with documentary programming certain filmic techniques, but it appears to have different goals: most notably, RTV aims to entertain more than inform and happily embraces the sensationalism that many documentarians avoid. There is on RTV no authoritative, objective exposition backed up by extensive research and rarely any advocacy or push for political reform. So if both types of programming portray intimate lives or everyday circumstances, it is generally for different ends. Their borders, however, are not clear and sometimes documentary is preserved as an evaluative rather than a logical distinction, whereby higher quality or more serious programming is accorded this status.

Finally, news programming might fairly be said to bear many resemblances to both RTV (on its infotainment and sensationalized end) and to documentary (when it comes to informing and addressing politics). The main contrast with reality TV would have to be that professional and reputable journalism eschews manipulation of material: whether it be staging, paying for contributions, or distortive editing – though it may be that the rise of reality TV problematizes and weakens the claims to objectivity of both documentary and news programming.

Is reality TV a genre?

Reality TV can be regarded as a recognizable category for purposes of discussion, marketing, and scheduling without it being a definite or universally agreed upon genre. The genre question has continued from RTV's inception right up through present day: from an impressive early discussion by Su Holmes and Deborah Jermyn (2004), to John Corner's concise overview (2010), to an excellent book-length study by Misha Kavka (2012). But while earlier commentators have been keen to identify reality TV as a genre or to underscore the difficulties in doing so, I won't spend time deliberating on this except to say that genres are discursive categories and matters of judgment. Today, the most common observation regarding genre in Literary or Media Studies is how fluid a concept it is and how difficult it is to pin down. Meanwhile, genre is often a pragmatic industry concern that determines both audience expectation and corporate investment as well as scheduling and distribution. While I will at times use "genre" as a useful shorthand for encapsulating a wide range of programming, I suggest that reality TV is defined more *ontologically* than *stylistically* and is best understood not so much as content with certain textual or aesthetic characteristics but as a relationship between texts, agents, and technical devices. It is, in other words, *a way of making television*. While particular topics or formats may trend only for a time, the basic production relations remain much the same – ordinary people, actual events, participation and interactivity.[3] Many see RTV as a good example of a hybrid genre or mega-genre that amalgamates other genres such as the game show, the talk show, the soap opera, the talent show, and the documentary. However, it may be wiser to discuss specific RTV *formats* – format being a subset of genre – as these are often distinct legal entities and commodities (unlike genres). Formats are defined by specific show elements: the shape and type of events (e.g., the form of competition or interpersonal interaction), the role of participants and hosts, the type of narrative, the subject matter. Yet as Jonathan Bignell (2005) points out, even formats are not always easily identified (hence legal disputes) and it depends if it is producers, participants, or viewers who are assessing these matters (p. 174).

Reality TV has proven to be highly resilient and has more than once been likened to a mutating virus (e.g., Gailey 2007: 108). Annette Hill describes RTV as a feral genre (2007) for being deterritorial, wildly opportunistic, and "resistant to containment" (p. 215). It has indisputably transformed television culture, mostly by leading the way in adapting to oncoming industry trends, among them: deregulation, privatization, increased commercial pressure (even on public broadcasting), proliferating niche channels, audience fragmentation, online interactivity, and global trade. RTV has spearheaded changes in production practices, subject participation, and the relation of text to audience. Its programming provokes strong reactions from viewers and has generated an extensive discursive field, both in mainstream media and viewer-generated content. People don't just watch reality TV: they blog about it, they read magazines and tabloids about it, they tweet about it. RTV is also striking for its demonstration of *glocalization* (locally adapted global phenomena) as its formats are often designed to be readily exportable and indigenized with local casts and content. This process often underscores the uneasy and continuing interplay between nationalism and globalism. Typically producers sell format details and provide creative consultants to go with them.[4] However, success is never predictable: for example, *Big Brother* and *Survivor* each fared differently in the relatively similar markets of the US and the UK. When formats travel further, they often challenge societal conventions, upsetting governments or religious authorities or different viewer demographics (more later). Even in original settings, RTV programming provokes more social controversies and debates than most other forms of television, due in some measure to its claims to represent reality and its use of real people. Programs make visible various areas of concern, from obesity to mental illness to criminality; but whether they deal with these in any prosocial or responsible manner is another matter.

Ethical concerns

Around the world, reality TV is both popular and held in low esteem. Even those who claim (with some pride) that they've never watched it tend to have strong as well as negative opinions about it. Some regard RTV as a debasement of television programming. It is framed as a distortion of documentary and a public service remit. In European contexts, evaluations of RTV are part of a larger discussion about whether the quality of TV programming has deteriorated since public service broadcasting lost some support and funding. The "crab grass" of television, RTV can be regarded as a cheap filler providing material for expanding commercial channels (Fishman 1998: 69). However, on both commercial and public channels there is, today, high-quality scripted programming as good as or maybe even better than in any previous era. So evidently RTV hasn't smothered this creativity, although its popularity has undoubtedly eliminated some opportunities for professional writers and performers.

But what about reality TV's moral influence on its audience? Journalistic and para-journalistic commentary[5] often becomes quite exercised about this matter and assumes RTV is indeed influencing individuals or society. It is also interesting to ask what it tells us about a society that it produces or watches so much RTV. In both instances I suggest speculation is legitimate but is just that: speculation. Even when parallels are found, it is important not to confuse *concurrence* (e.g., similar behavior occurring on screen and in real life) with *causality*. What we *can* demonstrate are the social debates and scandals this programming ignites in a wider cultural setting. Measuring specific viewers' responses (which is not quite the same as assessing broad cultural impact) is an important area of media research, but it is often limited by methodical and resource constraints: sample sizes, short durations, reliance on self-reporting, assumptions of immediate influence, and so on. Those who do it best acknowledge these restrictions. Also limited, but for different reasons, is the other approach which is for a single author to present an interpretation of media content based on textual analysis, with reference to others who have done likewise. This is essentially what I do here. It is what virtually all media scholars do, and their work is accorded worth if the interpretations appear to the reader to capture the local and wider significance of the content under analysis: that is, how this content may reflect, amplify, refract, model, or shape other cultural beliefs, techniques, or practices. Indeed, media analysis is valued as a means for elucidating or thinking through cultural trends as well as vice versa. It would seem reasonable to assume – based on the tenets of this broadly Cultural Studies approach – that an author's sociopolitical position and affiliations will inform their interpretation of content; however, some acknowledge this subjectivity more readily than others. The position I occupy is that of a White, mid-Atlantic, middle-class, liberal, professional female with more cultural than financial capital: a profile that is not particularly unusual in Media Studies.[6] When it comes to assessing the responses of other viewers, I do not attempt to offer anything prolonged or systematic. However, there is no question that viewers' online contributions (posts, blogs, tweets, recaps) are a valuable resource that I use as a base for gauging viewer reactions: unless otherwise stated, when I invoke viewer responses it is these sources I am drawing on. Indeed, I would argue that one of the things that makes reality TV worth investigating is the strong social response it generates, and so the relation between TV content and other platforms becomes the central focus of an upcoming chapter.

By the end of this book reality TV's cultural significance should come into focus but no definitive or causal linkages will be advanced. What media scholars *can* point to is how people on RTV behave, how they are portrayed and framed (textual cues), and how some viewers react (as reported on online posts, surveys, focus groups). But all of this information is circumscribed and a matter of interpretation. When it comes to ethics, it is also important to distinguish different possible areas of concern: the behavior of participants, the role of producers, the harm to viewers just by witnessing this behavior and, as a separate matter, concern that viewers will imitate unsavory behavior. Certainly, RTV is where social issues are represented and even tested, but what happens after that is difficult to determine. Commentators need to distinguish between content and impact, between RTV showing people behaving badly (in the opinion, say, of many viewers) and the influence this has on viewers (more difficult to demonstrate). For one thing, much depends on the social and psychological context out of which an individual viewer comes, and basic demographic data such as a viewer's age or gender barely touches on this. After studying audience responses to content, Katherine Sender (2012) concluded that journalists and media scholars may be overanxious about the influence of RTV (p. 77). Most of the time, if a series or type of series is popular, all we can say with certainty is that numerous people like to watch it – for reasons that they or others may not understand.

A common response is for people to report feeling shame or disappointment in themselves simply because they watch reality TV (e.g., Hill 2007: 201–2). Informal conversations begin somewhat defensively with "I don't watch reality TV" or "I hardly ever watch this stuff," after which the speaker often goes on to reveal some real familiarity with the programming or at least an awareness of its wider social currency. RTV is described as addictive, as crack TV, a guilty pleasure. Many viewers use the "train wreck" metaphor and say they find the shows appalling but can't look away. Often we witness a third-person effect where people acknowledge RTV's influence on others but not on themselves – whereas most sports fans have no such qualms and many viewers feel downright superior for watching documentaries. Later chapters will explore why viewers have such opinions, but when it comes to ethical influence we can say that RTV performs a useful function if nothing else because it inspires ethical debate and provides an opportunity to publicly calibrate what is considered admirable or disreputable behavior.

Plenty of advice and makeover formats are at base about good and bad behavior, but rarely do RTV participants or hosts explicitly invoke ethical principles or do more than critique individual incidents. On several docusoaps we get ethical deflection and deadpan avoidance: take the moral nullity of characters who when asked to assess a situation merely shrug and use the all-purpose "It is what it is," thereby closing off discussion of their culpability. Since its first appearance there have been claims that RTV encourages voyeurism, schadenfreude, mockery, lack of sympathy, and expectation of salacious or mean behavior. For some, RTV increases fears about a cheapening of experience: the emotions and ideas are too easy, simplistic, primeval, appealing to the lowest common denominator. RTV is too centered on unthinking pleasure, on sex, on greed. It shocks and provokes because it displays the unvarnished behavior of undisciplined young people or life-long extroverts. It encourages status-oriented consumption, narcissistic self-promotion, and basically doing anything for money. RTV normalizes an obsession with appearance, dysfunctional relationships, and rude behavior. It elevates shallow personalities and sanctions their excessive ambition, deception, selfishness, aggression and so on, so long as these lead to fame and fortune – as they sometimes do. However much any of this is true, there is no economic incentive in media entertainment to display only morally admirable behavior, and no accountability if it does not. Whether this is a good thing or not is another matter.

In general, it is important to recognize the *dramaturgical and commercial motives* of the broadcaster or producer and not assume too much about moral or ideological impact or intent. To draw an audience, producers feed off contemporary interests and concerns, but when we see greedy, selfish, or otherwise disreputable behavior, it doesn't mean they are deliberately promoting these values (as some commentators will complain). Yet, though direct influence may be impossible to establish, it may be easier to argue that, over time, the sheer prevalence of reality TV content on our screens may function to normalize certain values and behavior, some of which were previously disreputable or taboo.

As for the ethics of RTV production, there are concerns, too, about how participants are treated by producers. Does the programming unfairly trivialize, debase, or mock its subjects? Are some of its subjects so depraved that they deserve only public ridicule or are producers unfairly exploiting vulnerabilities and flaws (mental health issues, immaturity, fears, addiction, narcissism, and exhibitionism)? Is the participant's consent in all cases really informed and voluntary? Should children be involved? Does signing a contract make subjects fair game and privacy defunct? Should there be any monetary compensation? Do pressures and exposure lead participants to divorce, psychological harm, even suicide? These charges have all been made. In addition, I suggest there is a sadistic element, not always identified as such in academic writing, that links RTV to scripted entertainment. Subjects are regularly demeaned, humiliated, and sometimes undergo physical hardships or even basic food or sleep deprivation as well as the psychological trauma of harsh criticism and public rejection (even very young children). In other words, RTV is in tune with popular fictional drama where sadism is the last thrill used to attract jaded viewers. However, unlike fictional drama, RTV producers draw the line at murder – except in one case perhaps when in 2009 the producer of the Brazilian *Crimewatch* was accused of arranging for the murder of five people just to produce better ratings: police got suspicious when Wallace Souza's camera crews were always first on the scene.

Categorizing reality TV

Reality shows could be organized according to topic (cooking, home design) or according to format structure and dynamics (competition, docusoap). I believe the latter criteria are more useful because they more fundamentally identify how a format works and why it resembles or differs from other formats. For example, it is more characteristic of gamedocs (*Survivor; Top Chef*) to have a certain dramatic structure than a specific content: whether it involves food preparation or island survival, gamedocs build to one definite climax (elimination) with predictable prior segments (immunity challenges). Makeovers progress toward a final surprise revelation based on dramatic change, whereas docusoaps crosscut several ongoing narratives, interweaving the storylines of multiple characters. Many dynamics and protocols of reality TV are, not surprisingly, based on established genres: thus games become gamedocs, soaps become docusoaps, and sitcoms become what I will dub "comdocs." These combine the attraction of real people with the melodrama and resolution of scripted work. There are also less common variations on mystery/detective dramas (e.g., *The Mole*, ABC 2001–8) and more frequent adaptations of still recognizable genres like talent or cooking shows. Here the *RTV turn* often consists of adding more personal backstory, fraught interpersonal dynamics, and various degrees of competition. Whether game or docusoap, many RTV participants have to negotiate a *competitive and aspirational space* conceived of as a *market*.

It is important to remember that rather than there being viewers who like "reality TV," different viewers like specific and increasingly diversified series and do not like others. In the chapters that follow, I will at some points generalize about all of reality television and at others address characteristics found only in certain formats. RTV's address is wide: some series are designed to attract a very niche audience but others successfully attract a broad demographic and may be some of the few remaining examples of family programming (e.g., talent formats). My aim is to present a representative sample of major trends, focusing mostly on American and British programming. These are two close and cross-pollinating markets: with numerous American versions of British formats, British versions of American formats, in addition to directly imported programming, particularly of American RTV into Britain.

History

First, it is worth looking to see where reality TV has come from so we may better understand what it is. While it marks a distinct turning point in the history of television, RTV does have precedents in the earliest programming. Contemporary scholars have produced different schemas and, while there is no agreement about a definitive beginning, there is some consensus that reality TV grew out of a variety of prior formats and came into distinct formation by the end of the twentieth century. Valuable accounts of reality TV's history and origins can be found in Hill (2005), Bignell (2005), Biressi and Nunn (2005) and introductions to essay collections (e.g., Holmes and Jermyn 2004; Murray and Ouellette 2009). Misha Kavka's extensive genealogical model follows various twists and turns rather than producing a single narrative arc. Identifying no definite beginning point, she traces "multiple origins, intersections and resemblances" among RTV formats (Kavka 2012: 4). While I thoroughly recommend this detailed account, for purposes of a preliminary overview I will highlight significant trends within rough chronological periods, also identifying multiple roots and branches, and in the next chapter categorize programming according to fundamental ontological relations. As will become clear, many periods have dominant format types, although some individual series last a decade or more. Most commonly, formats appear, spawn imitations, and then quite rapidly disappear.

Most seeds of contemporary reality TV are found in the earliest forms of television: in instructional programming (cooking, gardening, home repair); in *Candid Camera* (from the 1947 radio show *Candid Microphone*); in quiz shows (*Queen For The Day*

1956–64; *Strike it Rich* 1951–8); and in talent competitions, some of which involved audience voting (*The Amateur Hour*, DuMont/ABC 1948–70; *Opportunity Knocks*, Thames 1956–78; *Come Dancing*, BBC 1949–98). By the 1960s and 1970s there was great social experimentation in life and in film (cinema vérité) and this inspired close scrutiny, fly-on-the-wall, domestic docusoaps like *An American Family* (PBS 1973), *The Family* (BBC 1974) and the still continuing *Up* series (ITV 1964–). These formats borrow from documentary an interest in social structures but foreground dramatic narrative and intimate personal revelations. Another embryonic form, a mix of people and commodity narratives, can be seen in the still running *Antiques Roadshow* (BBC 1979–; PBS 1997–).

In the late 1980s, significant technical innovations allowed mobile and nimble formats. This was the beginning of really light-weight cameras and small lav (lavalier) microphones that could attach to clothing. Closed-circuit TV surveillance also proliferated for law enforcement purposes, especially in Britain. Popular on TV was the ride-along *Cops* (Fox 1989–) and the mix of interview and dramatic reconstruction in *Rescue 911* (CBS 1989–96) and *999* (BBC1 1992–2003). *Unsolved Mysteries* (NBC 1987–97)[7] and *America's Most Wanted* (Fox 1988–) added to these law and emergency formats, what John Corner (2010) calls "the action route" that travelled from America to Europe,[8] and can be seen as part of a broader Reagan–Thatcher law-and-order culture (Kavka 2012: 46).[9] This was also the decade that saw the explosion of the talk show format, with its intimacy, humiliation, confession, and focus on ordinary people's emotional display. Another RTV precursor is the trend of infotainment and tabloidization, most noticeable in sensationalized news magazine programs like *A Current Affair* (Fox 1986–96). As with RTV later, both talk shows and infotainment gave air time to the otherwise marginalized, but preferred to frame them as shocking and deviant.

From the mid-1990s, easier editing software and digital equipment lowered costs and increased mobility further and by the end of the decade many recognizable RTV format types were now in place. Kavka (2012) describes 1989–99 as "the camcorder era" and designates it the first era of RTV. The term reality TV was in fact beginning to be used in the early 1990s to describe programming like *Rescue 911*. But more recognizable as what we now think of as RTV was *The Real World* (MTV 1992–), whose producers were inspired by *An American Family*. This was also the beginning of personal ritual narratives like *A Wedding Story* (TLC 1996–) and British workplace docusoaps such as *Airport* (BBC 1996–2005, 2008) and *Driving School* (BBC1 1997), what Corner (2010) distinguishes as the "daily life route" and Annette Hill as part of the second wave of RTV (2005: 24). Kavka (2012) notes the docusoaps' "closed ecologies" (p. 66) with regular staff and defined social structures and the focus on story and personality rather than serious journalistic probing. Also popular in Britain were lifestyle shows and makeovers of home and garden such as *Changing Rooms* (BBC 1996–2004, later *Trading Spaces*, TLC 2000–8), as well as skills competitions like *Masterchef* (BBC 1990–2001; 2005–) and *Ready Steady Cook* (BBC2 1994–2010). Inexpensive camcorders encouraged British access programming such as *Video Diaries* (1991–2) and *Video Nation* (1993–) where ordinary people sent in their recordings without any editorial intervention. Ordinary people also appeared in their own amateur videos on both sides of the Atlantic in *America's Funniest Home Videos* (ABC 1989–) and *You've Been Framed!* (ITV 1990–). In the US, they appeared as litigants in court shows (*Judge Judy*, 1996–) or in news magazines when captured by hidden cameras. Another technological development worth mentioning is the beginning of wide-scale web use in the late 1990s, something RTV producers were quick to exploit (chapter 3). As the 1990s came to a close, there was a burst of historical reconstructions in Britain and America beginning with *The 1990 House* (C4/PBS 1999),[10] and definitely less high-brow sensations on youth-oriented talent shows (*Popstars*, [NZ] 1999) and salacious docusoaps (*Ibiza Uncovered*, Sky One 1997, C4 1999).

The year 2000 marked the start of the first wave of full-blown reality TV as most use the term today. Suddenly and unexpectedly this programming was attracting high prime-time ratings, most notably the gamedocs *Survivor* (CBS 2000–) and *Big Brother*

(CBS, C4 2000–) once they were imported from Northern Europe to Britain and America in the summer of 2000.[11] These had in common: competition, total surveillance, short edit-to-air time-frame, and cross-media links. Soon after, these formats began to spread across the world (most notably *Big Brother*) and are still expanding today everywhere from Armenia to Vietnam. The emergence of this RTV was precipitated also by labor disputes in America: the writer's strike of 1988 had encouraged Fox to green light *Cops* and the threat of another strike boosted interest in reality TV in 2000. By 2001, reality TV had become an industry category recognized in the US TV Emmy Awards. It also greatly facilitated a rebranding of some American cable channels away from a more educational remit: for example, TLC used to be The Learning Channel, Bravo used to be a fairly high-brow (ad-free) arts and drama broadcaster, and the History Channel focused on historical archives (war footage). But by the new century, these channels began to broadcast more and more reality TV. Older formats like nature shows were repurposed by adding the RTV ingredients of extremism and sensationalism (*Animal Planet*). By now, traditional networks began to see some RTV series as tent poles[12] rather than fillers, with the success of *Survivor* and *The Amazing Race* for CBS (2001–) and *American Idol* (2002–) for Fox. Celebrity protagonists also caught fire from time to time, as with *The Osbournes* (MTV 2002–5) or *The Simple Life* (Fox 2003–5, E! 2006–7). In Britain there were impressive ratings for a variety of formats, from talent shows like *Pop Idol* (ITV 2001–3) and *The X Factor* (ITV 2004–), to celebrity vehicles like *I'm a Celebrity . . . Get Me Out of Here* (ITV 2002–), to makeovers like *What Not to Wear* (BBC 2001–7) and, above all, the blockbuster *Big Brother* (CBS/C4, C5 2000–).

In this period the makeover format became prominent and expanded in focus from home and garden to body and self, especially in the US. In some regards the makeover is an updated and more commercialized version of instructional programming, the new element being a focus on personal narratives and drama between host, participant, and viewer. RTV programming typically films people's *experience* of being instructed rather than actually attempting to instruct viewers (Couldry 2011a), but makeover formats enabled public service broadcasters to fulfill their educational remit with relatively little cost and often decent ratings. Different types of makeover soon emerged: style (*What Not to Wear*, BBC 2001–7; TLC 2003–13), style and décor (*Queer Eye*, Bravo 2003–7), home (*Extreme Makeover: Home Edition*, ABC 2003–12), lifestyle (*Made*, MTV 2002–), body (*Extreme Makeover*, ABC 2002–7), and then competitive makeovers (*The Biggest Loser*, NBC 2004–; *The Swan*, Fox 2004; *Ladette to Lady*, ITV 2005–10). Making over is also the basic dynamic in formats about career or business advancement (*Ramsey's Kitchen Nightmares*, C4 2004–9; Fox 2007–) or family life and parenting (*Supernanny*, C4 2004–11; ABC/Style, 2005–11). To some degree British TV demonstrates a greater interest in home makeovers and American TV in bodies; indeed, self-improvement is historically a more American preoccupation whereas the British not only take pride in their domestic "castles" but can restore any number of impressive historical buildings as part of a shared national heritage (*Restoration*, BBC2 2003–6). Some makeover formats have demonstrated real staying power: in the US, at the time of writing MTV's *Made* (2002–) and NBC's *The Biggest Loser* (2004–) are still going strong and *What Not to Wear* (2003–13) and *Extreme Makeover: Home Edition* (2003–12) recently ended after long runs and high ratings.

Another solid format that can run for multiple seasons is the dating competition, as seen in *The Bachelor* (ABC 2002–) and *The Bachelorette* (ABC 2003–). A more periodic but recurring hit is the faux format, especially popular in 2003 with *Joe Millionaire* (Fox 2003), *My Big Fat Obnoxious Fiancé* (Fox 2003–4), *The Joe Schmo Show* (Spike 2003–4; 2013). A hidden camera has also been embraced in a variety of ways, from *Punk'd* (MTV 2003–7, 2012) to *What Would You Do?* (ABC 2008). Some more physically torturous formats like *Fear Factor* (NBC 2001–6, 2011–12) had a good run, but overtly sadistic shows didn't fare too well (*The Chair*, ABC 2002; *The Chamber*, Fox 2002).

By the mid-2000s, a firmly established and reliable format was the talent show. For example, once the long-running *Come*

Dancing (BBC 1949–98) was dusted off, eroticized, and celebritized, it became a hit in Britain and America with *Strictly Come Dancing* (BBC1 2004–) and *Dancing with the Stars* (ABC 2005–). By mid-decade, many successful series were testing talents beyond singing and dancing, among them *America's Next Top Model* (2003–)/*Britain's Next Top Model* (Sky Living 2005–), *The Apprentice* (NBC 2004–; BBC2 2005–6, BBC1 2007–), *Project Runway* (Bravo 2004–), and *Top Chef* (Bravo 2006–). This period also saw the rapid rise of what I'm calling the American *luxury docusoap*, emphasizing glamour, leisure, and sexual display (*The Real Housewives*, Bravo 2006–; *Keeping Up with the Kardashians*, E! 2007–). Just prior to this MTV's affluent but more scripted docusoaps attracted a younger demographic: *Laguna Beach* (2004–6) and *The Hills* (2006–10), which later inspired *The Only Way Is Essex* (ITV2 2010–). There was also interest in expensive acquisition series like *My Super Sweet 16* (MTV 2005–8) and *Million Dollar Listing* (Bravo 2006–). In contrast is the emergence of rugged masculine shows involving adventure and hard labor (*Deadliest Catch*, Discovery 2005–; *Ice Road Truckers*, A&E 2007–), makeovers of motorbikes and automobiles (*Pimp My Ride*, MTV 2004–7) or competitive wheeling and dealing (*Pawn Stars*, History 2009–; *Storage Wars*, A&E 2010–).

Today, RTV programming appears across a wide range of channels, some of which are wholly dedicated to it.[13] Several specialize in certain demographics, such as young people (MTV), women (TLC, Lifetime), or men (History). Still popular, and the bread-and-butter of reality TV, are new or continuing gamedocs, talent and career competitions, and dating shows. Although a large turnover of programming is common, some series have been popular for over a decade: in the US, *Cops*, *The Real World*, *Big Brother*, *Survivor*, *The Amazing Race*, *The Bachelor*, *American Idol*, and *The Biggest Loser*. In Britain more stalwarts are *Celebrity Big Brother*, *The X Factor* and *I'm a Celebrity . . . Get Me Out of Here*. But while there are still new network hits like *The Voice* (NBC 2011–; BBC1 2012–) and shows that attract family audiences, many series attract smaller, niche audiences. RTV therefore suits narrowcasting and in many instances has enabled cable and satellite TV to flourish, allowing low-budget broadcasters to wall-paper schedules with inexpensive shows that don't quickly date and aren't celebrity driven.

Recent trends

One trend that is becoming noticeable is an evolution toward more *self-reflexivity*, especially as formats mature. There is today more internal acknowledgment that participants are on a TV show, that they know they have roles to play, businesses to promote, and viewer responses to consider. After a few docusoap seasons, the effect of being on TV becomes part of the content. Also, as part of this self-consciousness, we see a more heavy-handed scripting and storyboarding in docusoap and comedy formats, this in addition to more integration with online viewer activity.

Recently there has been a heightened fascination with the exotic and eccentric, whether in terms of wealth, class, culture, religion, or physical abilities. Viewers are invited to observe the Other, especially when they behave badly, without the impetus to improve or change them. Instead of charitable shows reaching out to help, wealth disparity is simply recognized and observed. Working-class figures, including groups that have not previously appeared much on TV (laborers, rednecks, gypsies), are now prevalent. Some series are quite sympathetic but many are mocking or at least ambivalent. Occasionally there are upper-class portraits or in the US simply high-end consumers. Either end of the economic spectrum works because RTV thrives on extremes and both the very rich and the very poor can behave with license. After the recession of 2008 there was some contraction (hence *Extreme Couponing*, TLC 2010–) but many series about entrepreneurship and business improvement survived this period and remain fairly buoyant (*The Apprentice*, NBC 2004–, BBC2 2005–6, BBC1 2007–; *Dragon's Den*, BBC2 2005–).

Gender specialization continues to demarcate men's and women's programming (more in chapter 5). Among series marked as feminine are numerous wedding-themed shows (these can be makeovers, gamedocs, or docusoaps), as well as style, family, and romance themes. Series with a masculine flavor often involve cars, tools, hunting, history, physical risk and adventure (man vs. nature). Noticeable, too, is an escalation in erotic display, especially by women. Countless docusoaps and competitions feature women in sexually charged poses and erotic dress: even in business settings a postfeminist sexualization seems to be de rigueur.

Building off the curiosity about different family arrangements in, for example, *Wife Swap* (C4 2003–9; ABC 2004–10) are more extreme examples in *19 Kids and Counting* (TLC 2008–) and *The Little Couple* (TLC 2009–). While these series are predicated on finding the abnormal, the framing is often quite sympathetic. Parents are admired for their resourcefulness in the face of hardship or (usually implicit) prejudice. More morbid is the increasing number of shows about individuals with pronounced psychological problems, such as *Celebrity Rehab* (VH1 2008–), *Hoarders* (A&E 2009–) or *My Strange Addiction* (TLC 2010–). The exoticism of religious subcultures is another contemporary draw: whether an *All-American Muslim* (TLC 2011–12), a polygamous Mormon family (*Sister Wives*, TLC 2010–) or Amish renegades (*Breaking Amish*, TLC 2012–; *Amish Mafia*, Discovery 2012–).

Reality TV and fictional drama

What we now recognize as reality TV was predicted in fictional film: for example, *Fahrenheit 451* (1966), *The Truman Show* (1998), and *EDtv* (1999). RTV, in turn, has influenced popular films such as *The Hunger Games* (2012). A few RTV shows have been loosely based on TV fictional drama: *The Real Housewives* on *Desperate Housewives*; *The Pitch* (AMC 2012–) on *Mad Men*; *The Glee Project* (Oxygen 2011–12) on *Glee*. But more significant is reality TV's impact on scripted drama. For example, several of TV's best comedies – *The Office* (BBC2 2001–3; NBC 2005–), *Arrested Development* (Fox 2003–6), *Parks and Recreation* (NBC 2009–), and *Modern Family* (ABC 2009–) – pretend to be a form of reality TV and borrow its *vérité* grammar (hand-held cameras, close-in shots, confessional interviews). More centrally, *The Comeback* (HBO 2005) was a fictional series about making a reality series. On *30 Rock* (NBC 2006–13) RTV's debasement of culture and of the media industry was a recurring theme: perhaps the most admired TV auteur of all, Aaron Sorkin (*West Wing*), made a cameo appearance to bewail RTV's decimation of professional writing positions (aired 3/24/11).[14] Meanwhile, references to the conventions of RTV and their integration into everyday life occur quite frequently in regular sitcoms: to take just a few examples, a mother on *The Middle* (ABC 2009–) is concerned about how bad they'd look if Jo Frost (*Supernanny*) were to visit, or characters on *It's Always Sunny in Philadelphia* (FX 2005–) expect free building supplies for a charitable project: after all, they argue, on RTV Sears doesn't demand payment and "they don't get anything from it!" (a dig at product placement).

Marketing and grammar

Once broadcast, reality series don't often sell well as DVDs or go into syndication and so economic pressures encourage rapid evolution and experimentation. With some enthusiasm, producers conceive narrative extensions (spin offs, sequels), franchise branches, revamps ("social editions"), meta-critical retrospectives (reunions), scheduling marathons, associated clusters (*The Xtra Factor*; *The X Factor 24/7*), or thinly disguised copies (*Wife Swap* vs. *Trading Spouses*). Derivative permutations are not a new idea in media entertainment, but they are particularly intense with RTV's multiple offerings each year. In fact, one can identify a grammar of reality show concepts and titles:

- Simple conjunction: *Redneck + Rehab = Redneck Rehab.* There can be more than two references in the combination: e.g., in *Texas Car Wars* all three terms summon up other series.
- Celebritization: *Celebrity + Apprentice = Celebrity Apprentice.*
- Conjunction and contraction: *Swamp People + Pawn Stars = Swamp Pawn.*

- Same prefix: *Redneck* – , *Million Dollar* – .
- Same suffix: – *Wars*, – *Kings*.
- Specification, typically location: *The Real Housewives of Atlanta* or *Storage Wars: New York*. This can be anticipatory also, as with *Princesses: Long Island* which constructs a place-holder for other possible locations.

Some of these formats generate spin-offs that evolve in a similar manner: e.g., from docusoap to talent show to makeover, where the star moves from surveillance subject to judge to expert. Thus *Cake Boss* (TLC 2009–) to *Next Great Baker* (TLC 2010–) to *Buddy's Bakery Rescue* (TLC 2013–); or *Dance Moms* (Lifetime 2011–), *Abby's Ultimate Dance Competition* (Lifetime 2012–), then *Abby's Studio Rescue* (Lifetime 2014). These are predicated on a particular star's rising cultural capital but follow the same trajectory.

Scholarly approaches

Reality TV poses important questions both for media scholars and for a wider public – some specific to RTV and many applicable elsewhere. But before investigating key topics, I offer an initial overview of current research.[15] RTV has quickly become a focus in Media Studies and to date there are about a dozen books and a similar number of edited collections devoted to this topic, in addition to scores of individual articles. The evolution of scholarly interests has depended to some extent on dominant programming. Essays first looked at early or proto forms of RTV such as crime shows, talk shows, and tabloid infotainment. When the major twenty-first-century wave hit, scholars were interested in comparing RTV series to documentary and engaged in debates about genre and ontological status. With gamedocs came concerns about surveillance and privacy, while makeover programming inspired discussions of neoliberalism, governmentality, and performativity: including performance of gender, race, and celebrity. Most recently, RTV scholarship has offered more comprehensive examinations of topics like class, affect, commercialization, and global politics. Further investigations of audience, genre, and political economy are also ongoing.

Main topics:
- representation: reality status, factual status, genre, genesis and growth of formats
- privacy, surveillance, intervention, governmentality
- commercialization, advertising, self-enterprise
- tabloidization, post-documentary, public service vs. commercial broadcasting
- identity, body, gender, class, race, sexual orientation
- celebrity
- politics, democracy, neoliberalism
- industry, political economy
- ethics, exploitation, voyeurism, debasement of values
- affect and viewer engagement
- globalization, nationalism
- technology, convergence, social media, new audience roles

Methods and publication types:
- predominantly textual analysis from a cultural studies perspective: e.g., how RTV content or practices represent a wider culture and its sociopolitical dimensions
- some audience research, employing focus groups, surveys, online viewer posts, and occasional ethnographic visits; also some participant studies and producer interviews (often legally restricted)
- some political economy: e.g., trade, regulation, casting, the economics of production
- some medium and technology studies: e.g., convergence, mobility
- some media effects studies from psychology or other social sciences: e.g., uses and gratifications, esteem, or body image impact
- several non-academic publications (also blogs, DVDs) outlining how to participate in or produce a show, as well as publications by successful participants (autobiographies, cookbooks)

In upcoming chapters I offer a broad synthesis of current thinking about reality TV. Each chapter brings the reader up to speed on a research area prominent in media studies, and those desiring more detail or depth in any particular topic are provided pointers for further reading. Limited space has necessitated condensation, but it is no judgment of the quality of any research if not included in my discussion.

Chapter 2 delves into the somewhat paradoxical concept of "reality TV" and includes a systematic assessment of what is or is not real about its production. The key attraction of "real" or previously unmediated people and their ordinary celebrity is also analyzed.

Chapter 3 underlines RTV's position at the forefront of cross-media distribution and its prefiguring of fundamental changes in the relations between participants, texts, and audiences, changes that are beginning to destabilize what is meant by "text" or "viewer" or even "television." As TV has become more open and dynamic, its producers have lost no time in commodifying viewer input. But there are countercurrents and complications also, as when paratextual (especially internet) activity creates some fascinating and sometimes subversive relations with the broadcast text.

Chapter 4 focuses squarely on the commercialization of reality TV and its role in a consumerist culture: both how this programming is produced and monetized, and the extent to which it promotes an ethos of consumption. This analysis encompasses new or revived forms of advertising, such as product placement, sponsorship, and online merchandising. Possible social ramifications include RTV's commodification of personal relationships (including with the self) and its contribution to the destabilizing of a concept as fundamental as privacy.

Focusing on representations of gender, sex, and race, chapter 5 demonstrates RTV's proclivity for capitalizing on the stereotypical and the abnormal for comic or morbid effect. Of academic interest are its accessible portraits of postmodern or post-traditional ideas about malleable identities and the self-as-project. Taking gender, sexual orientation, and race/ethnicity in turn, this chapter examines types and degrees of representation and considers topics such as: gendered programming, consumption and identity, body imagery and management, lifestyle, mainstreaming, depoliticization, and the selling of diversity.

A consideration of social markers continues in chapter 6 with a focus on class. Often erased or taboo elsewhere, its strong presence on reality programming allows us to consider contemporary views about class and their role in entertainment. On RTV the perspective is generally middle-class, but there appears to be room for mockery of any class, or rather caricatures of any class.

Chapter 7 offers a general account of RTV and politics, the aim being to examine both implicit and explicit political content. This discussion highlights scholarly interest in surveillance, governmentality, neoliberalism, globalism/nationalism, and democratization. In some instances RTV has had a direct effect on politics (government or citizen action), and even more rarely intends to have this kind of effect (e.g., nutrition reform), but more typically producers avoid a political address – which is not to say that ideological work isn't being done, as any media scholar will point out.

2

Reality Status

"We all know that reality shows are to real life what Pringles are to the potato"[1]

On any given day in the world of reality TV, people are plotting around a campfire, entering a talent contest, competitively racing through foreign lands, planning a wedding, designing clothes, getting drunk, punching roommates, inviting parenting/design/ relationship experts into their home, swapping wives, consulting mediums, playing tricks on strangers, swimming in mud, and going on dates arranged by TV producers/offspring/professional matchmakers. Some of these things also typically happen to ordinary people in real life, but not all. So at once a basic distinction arises between ordinary events and TV shows. Most viewers recognize the difference, but it is not a straightforward one. Indeed, one attraction of reality television is that it muddies and plays with the distinction between event and program, between real life and representation: in fact RTV has put so much stress on the notion of reality that we may now be at the point of referring to "real reality." This chapter examines the kind of reality embedded in reality TV and asks: if it is indisputably TV, in what ways is it also "reality"? In making this determination we will learn a good deal about this programming's aims and conventions.

There is no doubt that reality TV's provocative name and status are what intrigue many viewers – just as producers hoped it would. Its self-conscious claim suggests there is some special and novel relation to "reality" that constitutes its brand identity. But in critiquing this marketing strategy people like to ask: Is "reality TV" a misnomer? An oxymoron? I will argue that there is no absolute yes or no answer to these or similar questions. The title's yoking of reality and television has some validity. The aim of this chapter is to consider both terms and judge what is staged and what is not. One might say that RTV turns reality into Reality, into almost a proper noun, a location, a tradable commodity – for this and other reasons we might more accurately refer to Reality TV (I and some others used this form a decade ago but the lower case version has now become the norm).[2] As a concept, "real" can mean different things – actual, authentic, genuine, unexpected, raw, autonomous – and RTV programming can claim several of these distinct elements. Ask instead how real*istic* is this programming and this introduces a concept almost as slippery as real. Generally a measure of how convincing, probable, or verisimilar a representation is (i.e., how it is perceived), realism concedes a fictionality and lack of non-fictional veracity that may not fit either. Another modest but dizzying claim is to consider what kind of *reality effect* RTV creates (Black 2002; also Boorstin 1992 [1961]; Baudrillard 1983). My approach, however, is to put weight on referential meaning, on the actual status of the referents. Judgments about plausibility of behavior or verisimilitude remain more subjective and viewer-dependent.

Defining reality TV

As a TV category, reality TV has variously been described as non-scripted drama, non-fictional programming, dramality, and factual entertainment.[3] Factual entertainment strikes me as appropriate when factual indicates something actually occurring at a particular place and time, not necessarily objectively represented or scientifically verifiable. Clearly RTV adopts some conventions of fiction – shaping (but not wholly composing) stories and characters, encouraging melodrama, employing emotive music, cliffhangers, dramatic irony, red herrings, and so on – but none of these place it in the category of the imaginary. We can identify a spectrum within fiction from *wholly imagined* and fantastic/ impossible in real life to *very plausible though made up*; then in non-fiction, from highly contrived situations and a *heavy shaping* of material to an *exact observation* of actual events unaffected by their recording. Much RTV appears to occupy the middle of the non-fictional range where the distinction between happening in actuality and being imagined remains. Through advanced story-boarding and casting, TV producers can construct conditions and try to determine drama that editors then shape into narratives. But encouraging or shaping drama is not the same as wholly imagining it. Perhaps RTV can be thought of as *synthetic*, meaning an amalgam manufactured or created in an artificial process but not actually or materially unreal. It is fabricated only in the sense of made, not made *up*.

To say that reality TV merely records reality is obviously too simplistic, but so is saying it is all false. Clearly there are relatively unprocessed and raw elements in reality TV and many formats are genuinely aleatory and unplanned up to a point, though these real elements are generally "managed" (to pick a fairly neutral term) in order to be profitable, dramatic entertainment. It is the mix of the spontaneous and the planned that draws an audience, not the raw or real alone. Surveys suggest that what interests viewers is what Katherine Sender (2012) incisively encapsulates as RTV's "uneasy location between transparency and artifice" (p. 107). One way of understanding this location is as a social *experiment* in the sense of an environment with many controlled variables, though not with specific hypotheses or falsifiable results. Early on, some RTV, most notably *Big Brother*, was presented as just such an experiment, but this rationale soon faded away along with the hired psychologists. Still, this doesn't mean experiment is an invalid way of thinking about much RTV in a larger sense of setting up parameters, letting things happen, observing them, then communicating and inter-preting results. Indeed, John de Mol's inspiration for *Big Brother* was the real scientific experiment of Biosphere 2.[4] Also productive is Kevin Robins' early description of "karaoke television" (1996: 140), which underscores the combination of professional structure (soundtrack and lyrics) and amateur and not always predictable input. Along the same lines, RTV could be accurately described as a form of improvisation that encourages structured spontaneity. More specifically, many formats could be regarded as forms of play, a mode between pretend and real/natural that also combines structure and spontaneity.

However, for most purposes, I believe the most accurate and useful descriptor is what I have termed "staged actuality" (Deery 2012), drawing on both meanings of staged as planned and as performed (see also Piper 2004: 276). Actual is employed in the most basic sense of real-life and real-time empirical occurrence and is a useful bedrock term for making more modest claims than "real."[5] Misha Kavka and Amy West (2004) underline that the etymology of "actual" is related to a temporal sense of now, rather than an ontological claim to truth. Hence the channel truTV, whose RTV formats sometimes use paid actors and scripts, can still claim they present "Not reality. Actuality." RTV events take place in a real time and place, but there will be different mixes of contrivance and spontaneity before, during, and after filming. The conjunction of empirical event and media staging is fundamental, but the degree and type of staging will vary – with only one constant, that most of it will remain hidden. Hence RTV viewers are often actively engaged in judging who or what is real or true. Going back and forth between suspicion and trust seems to be part of the viewing experience and, while frustrating for some, this spectator sport has proven to be a primary pleasure (e.g., Hill 2005). Extending this further, it could be that reality TV foregrounds the increased difficulty of knowing what is true or unbiased or disinterested in wider society – in large part due to media saturation and to the rhetorical masking of much commercial and political discourse (Deery 2012). For Mark Andrejevic (2004: 223), RTV demonstrates the inadequacy of the concept of reality and caters to the savvy awareness that reality is contrived and largely mediated.

Nevertheless, reality TV helps illustrate the difference between two kinds of unreal: the fake and the fictitious. With fiction, an author is admired for making things up. But not so in news or documentary and nor, it seems, on reality TV – in fact, RTV is not supposed to be authored at all. RTV gets close to fictional drama when we recognize that its participants perform roles to varying degrees, but the actor in fictional drama is known to be pretending to be someone else and the illusion is innocent, whereas RTV performances can be judged fake or deceptive. One way to consider the authenticity or fakeness of RTV is according to different relationship coordinates: we can judge how genuine or honest *participants* are being to viewers, to each other, or to producers; or how honest *producers* are in relation to viewers, participants, or other members of the production staff. The permutations are complex. For instance, when it comes to producers we can ask: How much is the situation and premise staged and contrived? How much does editing manipulate and create? Are the producers being forthright and honest with the participants before and during filming? We can ask of participants: to what extent are they performing for the camera? Is their individual or group behavior like it is in everyday life off screen? Are they deceiving each other? And so on.

Without opening up a full-blown metaphysical discussion of the concept of the real or the determination of its status, this chapter will outline the more raw and the more staged aspects of RTV programming. Viewers will make different judgments about the reality claims of each show: even with "fly-on-the-wall" filming it is worth remembering that a fly's vision has many facets, as do those who produce or watch a TV show. But I suggest that RTV typically produces something between the truth and the whole truth: people did utter the lines that appear in the broadcast, but they also said a great deal more and the selection and ordering of snippets can give an ultimately false or partial impression. My contention is that while it furthers creating impressions, selling lifestyles, and iconicizing the hollow and flawed – all key features of late modernity – reality TV also answers a nostalgic desire for the authentic.[6] It can be seen as symptomatic of today's distant intimacy, its mediated sociability, and the confessions, memoirs, or rehabilitations whose transparency attracts attention but may not guarantee truth. Still, people like to flirt with it and viewers report being excited when they spot it – the truth.

Real elements

We can start with the claim that reality TV is *a non-fictional presentation of actual events occurring in the empirical world as experienced by amateur participants who have not been hired to act as someone other than themselves or to recite a program-length script.* One could argue further that the most important thing about reality TV is that it is not fictional: that this is why it entertains and impacts our culture in a different way than fictional texts. Viewers are attracted to people "being real," to raw emotions, surprises, unpredictable outcomes. RTV programming is indexically linked to actual referents that occur in front of the camera, not computer generated special effects. It also presents real experiences in the sense of physical challenges or emotional stresses that produce tangible physiological responses such as blushes or tears, indexes that are read as evidence of genuine feeling (e.g., Sender 2012: 115). Its repertoire includes experiences as real and generally uncontrived as birth or death. Another dimension of the realness of RTV is its real-life consequence. The impact a show has on participants and their social relations is generally more immediate and intense than if simply acting a fictional role.

Outside celebrity series, reality participants are considered ordinary or "real" (both terms are often used interchangeably) because they are not professional actors performing a scripted role.[7] Laura Grindstaff (2014) suggests that RTV participants are "performing performance" in that they dramatize how we all project and perform in real life. They make conscious the usually unconscious, habitual performances of every day. Indeed, RTV participants may be modeling a broader trend toward performativity in numerous occupational, political, and cultural fields where, increasingly, displaying performative competence becomes a form of cultural capital and therefore power (Grindstaff 2014: 341). In playing themselves in a mediated setting RTV subjects also resemble, and may have anticipated, much online activity (Andrejevic 2014). But when RTV viewers acknowledge that everyone performs in everyday life (even when not mediated), they look for an on-screen performance that more resembles this level of acting than a stage actor's impersonation of someone else; this, of course, requires speculation and empathy on the viewer's part (Hill 2005: 69).

If there is no strict border between amateur and professional performance, RTV producers nevertheless emphasize amateur status. They seek applicants who have not appeared on screen before and stipulate how often they can reappear in future shows. Indeed, one of the cultural shifts that reality TV encourages is the recasting of *ordinary* as *previously unmediated*. In a typical Release Form recipients must attest that: "My participation in the casting process for the Program, and in the Program itself, do not constitute a performance and will not entitle me to wages, salary, or other compensation."[8] However, this is not universal: some formats now pay participants a sizeable income and may employ people with previous acting experience. Still, the distinction is that if they are playing a role it is themselves – or perhaps versions of themselves ranging from heightened and self-edited to the caricatured. Hence we might describe some RTV subjects as *figures*, somewhere between real-life and fictional characters. Derek Kompare refers to them as "constructions of personality" (2004: 111) and Leigh Edwards astutely observes that instead of fiction trying to make characters seem real, RTV turns real people into characters (2013: 17).

Even when cast to play a type, there is a certain amount of indeterminacy. Producers often do not know how interpersonal relations will evolve and have to make the most of the way the subjective viewpoints of viewers and players shift. When all parties are bombarded by ambiguous signs they have to try to negotiate, this encourages a high degree of audience engagement. In gamedocs a player's "alliance" (a word now overlaid with dubious RTV associations) can be regarded as an agreement to share – or pretend to share – the same perspective and interpretation, but these coalitions prove ephemeral and unpredictable. In addition, audience input such as voting creates further indeterminacy.

Staged Elements

We could say that reality TV is to real life as ice is to water: it is the same substance but is transformed and available for further shaping. The intricacy and type of sculpting varies from format to format, but there are some common practices.

Pre-production

We can start with the fundamental idea that on RTV events often occur only *because* they are being filmed. They are, in other words, *pseudo-events* – defined by Daniel Boorstin as paid for, planned, dramatic, easily understood, conveniently distributed, and advertised in advance (Boorstin 1992 [1961]: 39–40). Like much else in our public and even private life, mediation is their reason for being. Beyond this, the process of mediation affects participant behavior and creates a perturbation effect, as when the physicist's observation affects subatomic behavior. Since *An American Family* the ethics of this effect has been debated; for example, HBO's film *Cinema Verite* (2011) portrays director Craig Gilbert pressuring participants to generate drama and his camera crew's disapproval. Some attempts have been made to reduce the physical camera's presence, as on recent "precinct TV," where largely hidden and remotely controlled miniature cameras are installed in a public institution to unobtrusively record personal lives (*One Born Every Minute*, C4 2009–). Described by its broadcasters as observational documentary, the expectation is that when less aware of being filmed subjects will behave more authentically (Bignell 2014).

However, in most formats, factors like dramatic conventions, legal constraints, financial limits and target audiences, affect how someone behaves and is portrayed on TV. Casting, too, shapes future content. As a form of pre-production scripting, casting selects characters whose narratives may be shaped to produce at least some predetermined effects.[9] Sometimes the process is itself part of the drama: as in *Idol* auditions. Outside talent shows, casting creates inauthenticity when producers attract those who want to be on TV but then expect these people to hide this motive, hence applicants often present as unambitious non-actors when in fact they are trolling for a chance to publicize themselves. Docusoaps suggest that cameras record informal friendship networks but actually producers select participants (even if recommended by other participants). What stretches credulity is when new cast members act as though they have never before seen the show or appeared in other shows, whereas numerous participants are by now recirculating within the RTV plane of existence. Some are caught self-consciously performing an induced or fake role, as when *Breaking Amish* subjects pretended to be newly emerging ingénues but were later discovered to be already established in mainstream culture. Even when not directed in this way, there has to be at least some legal prepping of show participants who need to be briefed on defamation and privacy laws and sign release forms. Cast members also often have stylists and make-up artists who visually prep them, just like professional actors.

Nevertheless, it is important at this point to recognize the distinction between narrative and fiction. Shaping actual events into a narrative is not the same as fabricating fiction out of whole cloth. Still, RTV producers do often have storyboards or prefabricated outlines of how they think the action will unfold, with anticipated character exchanges and events. Many series borrow standard dramatic plots, such as 30 or 60 minutes of *conflict – disorder – resolution*, and cast members are expected to perform consistent roles to further this plot. Indeed, RTV has been around for so long that its formats have recognizable conventions, so even raw action can be somewhat predictable for viewers and participants. Beyond television (although influenced by it), producers are happy to leverage conventional social structures with broad scripts such as courtships, weddings, or births. Other shows use economic systems to construct drama, as when even apparently fly-on-the-wall productions like *The Deadliest Catch* or *Storage Wars* mold the broader competition of capitalism into a personal rivalry.

On some series the whole premise can be fake and deceptive. For example, on *Parental Control* (whose camp artificiality is examined by J. Gray 2009), producers apparently pick people who aren't dating, put them in a house they don't actually live in, and make them say ridiculous things. Similar claims have been made about *House Hunters* (HGTV, 1999–) where couples report that when chosen for the show they have already bought a home and so pretend to look at houses actually belonging to obliging friends and family (White 2014). Former participants on *Restaurant Stakeout* (Food Network 2012–) also claim that producers hire actors to act as staff members in order to create more dramatic scenes.

TV producers anticipate drama, find drama, heighten drama, or induce drama. *The Simple Life* is an early example of unacknowledged scripting even at the sentence level, creating what its producers called a "hybrid sitcom."[10] On such shows producers manage situations, provide lines, or ask subjects to come up with scenarios that will be worth filming. The cast is knowingly or unknowingly manipulated in multiple ways in order to produce the desired narrative; in contrast to paid and professional actors who are more directed but are in many ways less manipulated. A former contestant on *The Bachelorette* learned that there were writers assigned to work on a plot line for each character (Bussewitz 2011). Meanwhile RTV veteran Jack Benza claims that on one show producers planned the order people would be eliminated and the cast began to guess this and resist (2005: 144). Certainly, many formats are known to be at least partly scripted in advance: intros, interview questions, narrator's voiceovers, and the host's patter if nothing else.

On other occasions cast members of their own initiative orchestrate scenes independently of producers, though this can backfire. One former docusoap star (*The Real Housewives of New York City*) admitted she picked a fight because she thought it would make "great television," but she underestimated the real hurt feelings and alienation it caused both viewers and cast and, possibly as a result, she was fired. Viewer consternation and disgust also erupt when it is believed that participants are staging or manipulating their own life narratives simply to make good ratings, a prominent example being Kim Kardashian's second wedding and quick divorce.

Occasionally there are official hoaxes, the first being *The Joe*

Schmo Show, where producers mix paid actors and scripts with an ordinary and oblivious "mark." Later, the rather elaborate *Space Cadets* convinced participants they were going into space while they sat in a simulated shuttle and studio set costing $7 million. *Bedsitcom* (C4 2003) mixed ordinary participants and (unknown to them) actors who were being fed lines. Other shows offer misleading information to some cast members to add a wrinkle to the competition (*Tool Academy*, VH1 2009–10, E4 2011; or *Joe Millionaire*). Some of the best descriptions of the RTV aesthetic appeared in the fictional satire *30 Rock*. One episode incorporated all the conventional elements of hand-held cameras, fast transitions, crude cast descriptions, bleeps, blurred faces, hair pulling, wine throwing, and advertising one's own business. The writers' mockery was a testament to RTV's now established presence. Hoaxes like *The Joe Schmo Show* also acknowledge and mock RTV archetypes and rituals. They provide viewers some glimpses of the challenges and motives behind RTV's mediation of reality and so ultimately they are shows about the making of reality TV shows, and, more broadly, the representational practices of the television industry (Hearn 2009). *Joe Schmo* satirizes formulaic and ludicrous conventions, but it also relies on the fact that by now people can believe anything of RTV. This was illustrated by a US public television fundraising campaign with trailers for spoof RTV shows like *Knitting Wars*, with the tag line: "The fact you thought this was a real show says a lot about the state of TV. Support quality programming" (WNET 2013). Other formats with a behind-the-scenes dimension are sting operations like *Punk'd* or *Bait Car* (truTV 2007–) where viewers are shown the process of staging. While there are no formal rehearsals (outside talent shows), in some RTV formats crews practice games or scenes before participants show up and field producers rehearse camera angles.

Filming

RTV is a small world. In the US it mostly encompasses New York City and Los Angeles, not coincidentally the twin headquarters of the media industry. RTV locations are generally selected or constructed to produce high physical or psychological stress. This stress may include food or sleep deprivation: i.e., practices that are otherwise regarded as forms of torture. Another approach is to influence behavior through (apparent) reward or gratification: for example, by plying subjects with alcohol or transporting them to luxurious (but shared) accommodations. To reduce costs, already extant locations are revamped to create a particular *mise-en-scéne*, so hotels pose as "retreat centers" or conference centers are presented as "finishing schools." Moving locations is another source of drama. On docusoaps producers invariably encourage the cast to go on (paid for) vacations where the close quarters create high drama. Producers usually set up social events and provide transportation (hence the prevalence of limos).

While reality TV reveals some of the reality of TV production (depending on how savvy and media literate the viewer is), there is a good deal of official suppression of this staging. Cameras occasionally film the presence of other cameras, perhaps to add to the aesthetics of liveness and ambush (*Repo Games* or *Catfish*), but ordinarily the camera crew does not appear in broadcast material unless inadvertently and fleetingly in a mirror or as a shadow. There are occasional ruptures in the more self-reflexive reunion shows when participants storm off the set and viewers get glimpses of a sizable production staff. But neither those producing nor those appearing on RTV say much about casting or other economic arrangements; not surprising given the tight contracts and enforced code of silence on these matters (some of which stipulate "in perpetuity and throughout the universe"). Cloaking the production process has obvious economic advantages – most centrally, it attracts viewers by promising the real or raw, but it also helps maintain suspense, controls the marketing of the program, and allows producers to avoid having to disclose generally poor working conditions.

No one on screen acknowledges that they are on a show, yet many of the conventions of fictional filming are there: including scenes of people sitting round a table but leaving a gap so no one's back is to the camera. One could say that RTV is inherently inauthentic because it asks people who know they are being filmed to act as if they are not being filmed and in this sense to "act natural" (the assumption being that natural equals unmediated). The fourth wall is ignored, not to protect the illusion of fiction but to protect the *illusion of non-fiction*. Even on *Big Brother* the cameras are hidden though all know they are present. Contestants sometimes speak directly to the camera and try to have a relationship with "Big Brother," especially in the UK version. Some critics suggest this hypermediated format produces a more authentic program because participants acknowledge the cameras are there in their "house"/set and, because there is a total surveillance, participants must sooner or later drop their masks. Similarly, *The Real World* claims to be about "what happens when people stop being polite and start getting real."

As a strategy in the competition, however, participants do perform front-stage and back-stage selves (Goffman 1959), both to each other and to the viewers (Kavka 2012: 96).[11] Elsewhere, the production crew occasionally participates in the situations they cover, especially on multiple series with children who have not yet learned to ignore the cameras. Parents have been criticized for exposing young children to this kind of surveillance. Others criticize them when they don't. For example, some docusoap mothers are criticized for apparently neglecting their children because they rarely appear with them, when often this is attributable to them protecting their children's privacy. Viewers forget the distinction between RTV and real life. Occasionally, in a crisis, subjects break the usual arrangements, as in Jade Goody's final days when she asked producers to assist her, or when the TV crew pitches in on *The Deadliest Catch*, or an angry docusoap diva yells at the camera crew to stop filming and shoves them out of the way. However, most often the film crew remains unseen and uninvolved. This is the case even when criminal or dangerous actions are taking place. They are not legally obliged to intervene and they generally don't.

Economic scripting

Needless to say, economic interests shape participant behavior. A big incentive on ensemble docusoaps is renewal of contract. Hence, as "friendships" unravel people nevertheless continue to meet and what could be passed off as generosity of spirit is much more likely pressure from producers. Giving people who might not otherwise do so an incentive to congregate, and whenever possible plying them with alcohol, is almost guaranteed to create drama; RTV's common strategy being to provide people enough rope to hang themselves. The content participants are encouraged to create (conflicts, fights) therefore wears away at the ontological premise of the show: that it is a documentary-style filming of peoples' freely chosen activities, not obligated meetings under contract.

Producers evidently judge the worth of most cast members dramaturgically, not ethically. Even when claiming to find people best suited for a certain career they often favor drama over identifying realistic job skills: as with 5-minuite culinary masterpieces (*Top Chef*) or acrobatic feats (*Next Top Model*). However, participants and viewers don't always agree with this priority. In *The Glass House* (ABC 2012), for instance, one contestant revealed that he intended to play the villain to generate drama and entertain viewers. When another contestant protested: "you have no character!" (meaning moral character), he proudly replied "I am the only character on this show!" (meaning entertaining). Despite this, viewers swiftly voted him off.

Interviewing and bargaining

In individual on-the-fly (OTF) interviews the real and the actual are provoked, agitated, and stimulated, if not simulated. Off-camera interviewers glean information from participants and then feed information to others in the hopes that it will stir the pot. They steer participants to talk about certain issues or emote something that will contribute to a desired narrative, even displaying the emotions they wish the interviewee to imitate. When a subject breaks down and cries on camera their conventional apology is misdirected – illustrating the difference between ordinary social conventions and RTV. Interviewers may use the subject's fears and insecurities against them; for example, employing racist comments to make this the upcoming theme (Benza 2005: 63–4). Some formats resemble interrogations where stress or deprivation is used to produce raw emotion and candor. Alternatively, producers may offer incentives like food or (ironically) media access to get subjects to do or say something. Participants themselves may barter with producers (Pozner 2010: 101) or make secret deals with the film crew. A Danish *Big Brother* cast went on strike and won concessions like private time and family visits, while participants on *I'm a Celebrity* won better food (Bignell 2005: 24). During regular filming, the crew's presence puts implicit pressure on participants to do or say something dramatic. Their yawning, sighing or eye rolling can be forms of "emotional management" designed to illicit a response (Grindstaff 2011a: 50).

One clue that action is pre-planned is when multiple cameras and lights are already in position before a supposedly surprise event takes place. Some scenes are also immediately re-enacted if the first take is not successful: apparently this happens fairly frequently on makeovers and gamedocs. A brief scene might take hours to shoot (observant viewers can sometimes see the light change from day to night). On dating and docusoap formats there are reconstructions of missed shots or mumbled lines; e.g., one *Real Housewives* show runner says in his blog: "During interviews, we'll often ask cast members to repeat their answers if they stumble while speaking them."[12] Some producers will stop the action if something good is not currently being caught on film and ask participants to continue once the cameras are on, even to the point of making someone dry their clothes and get wet again (Benza 2005: 54, 138). Some field producers direct participants through an ear-piece as the action unfolds but this may be more common in formats like dating shows and gamedocs (Caudle 2011: 121).

Live broadcasting, utilized most in talent shows and gamedoc finales, is the ultimate fulfillment of reality TV's aesthetic of immediacy. Although there may have been some shaping of material prior to filming, viewers and participants are conscious of experiencing something "together" because, at the same moment, this synchronicity produces a more real and intimate effect (Kavka and West 2004)[13] – although the attraction of much reality TV may remain the simultaneous sense of being there (it is so real) but also of *not* being there (that is a comfort) (Baudrillard 1998 [1970]: 34). For participants, some formats encourage an alternative reality bubble: social groups become focused and intense, sometimes provoking viewers to remark that players need a "reality check," meaning an awareness of how their TV experience compares to their behavior in everyday life. Participants are indeed shocked on re-entry and many a TV romance withers when it emerges from the greenhouse effect of well-lit sets.

Finally, it is worth noting that filming styles shape viewer perceptions. Unstable hand-held camera footage has long been used to suggest deeper intimacy and immediacy, the sweeping panoramics of *Survivor* attempt epic (or at least documentary) grandeur, whereas the grainy and maybe nostalgic interstitials of *Jersey Shore* (MTV 2009–12) flirted with the series' hybrid nature as both raw and staged. Whether these or other stylized visuals have the effect of making things seem more authentic or more contrived is an interesting question.

Editing

Clearly, editing is a form of post-production scripting in which selection is interpretation (e.g., Miller 2006: 113). On RTV there are often high shooting ratios of 100:1 or even 300:1 (one hour broadcast from 300 hours of shooting). One RTV producer likens editing to an adaptation: "It's the story person that whittles a 90-minute dinner down to a 3-minute scene, just like a screenwriter adapts an 800-page novel into 120 pages of script."[14] *Survivor* allows several months for post-production work, *Big Brother* a few days, and live broadcasts none at all. Sometimes story editors will splice different snippets of conversation ("Frankenbites") or reaction shots to construct an interaction that did not actually occur. Often editing is used to construct characters, making some figures more villainous and others more virtuous than a more comprehensive picture would reveal. Other editing is used to preserve suspense; so when editors know who is going to be expelled next, they can highlight why this was likely or obfuscate and plant red herrings. Viewers are shown clips out of sequence to create a dramatic effect or information can be time released to maximize drama. Some editing is more *editorial* than others and more inclined to make an observation, show disapproval, or undermine subjects, as when a pageant mother's "I only do it because my kid loves it" is interlaced with shots of the same child declaring she hates it. Direct voiceovers are infrequent (a notable exception is the sneering commentary on *Bridezillas*), but other reaction cues can come from music and soundtracks.

One dubious area of editing is when shows make claims about what can't be seen at all, as with ghost hunters and mediums. The essentially non-falsifiable claim to communicate with the dead may depend not only on quick thinking on the medium's part but also selective editing. Witnesses at live readings claim editors of *Long Island Medium* (TLC 2011–) omit false guesses to create a more convincing authenticity and my own experience at a live show backs this up, although the instant repurposing of false assertions was impressive. On the TV show, there is no editorial voiceover but it does seem produced in such a way as to bolster the psychic's truth claims and therapeutic effect. At the live event (in a theatre seating over two thousand), audience members were repeatedly warned that recording the performance was prohibited, presumably to preserve the TV show's more impressive record.

Reception

If few viewers see RTV as offering a fully transparent reality, this does not mean they aren't interested in ways in which it *is* real, factual, or true, and while on the philosophical level we can wonder to what extent any representation can ever be any of these things, on the production level viewers can speculate about how producers or participants are manipulating material and according to what agenda. Reality TV allows viewers to become absorbed in the drama and suspend critical judgment of its processing of real events, or enjoy critiquing its artifice – or both. British research- ers Skeggs and Wood (2009, 2012) have found middle-class viewers to be more critical and aware of producer manipulation than working-class viewers, whereas Sender (2012) found in her sample that US viewers were savvy across all classes. She found many "media-reflexive" viewers who were aware of the staging, the editing, the casting, and genre expectations. Hence, as scholars have noted, one of the ways RTV is significant is its promotion of media literacy (e.g., Hill 2007: 133–4, 164–6; Andrejevic 2008). However, while many viewers recognize that contrivance is used to make actuality more entertaining, they value and try to locate the real and the raw (Hill 2005, 2007). Even when participants are openly performing, as on talent shows, audiences and judges still reward those who seem to emote genuine feelings as they sing. Nick Couldry has made a fundamental point that people think of the media as privileged sites for accessing social realities, and so in the case of reality TV we can't just discount the "reality" in the title: it is not just a dead metaphor and it does affect audience expectations (Couldry 2011a: 194–5). Certainly, surveys suggest that viewers put emphasis on how much a reality show is factual or true and classify shows accordingly. Annette Hill (2005) found that "an ethic of truth telling is by far the most common type of criteria used to judge the quality of popular factual programming as a whole" (p. 174) and that "[t]he more fictionalised factual pro- gramming becomes, the less viewers value it" (p. 175).

That reality TV is significant for making us think about per- formance and authenticity on screen and off is underlined in an impressive and comprehensive discussion by Skeggs and Wood (2012) who, with other media scholars, relate TV roles to funda- mental issues, concerns, and confusions in contemporary identity formation. Audience studies indicate that viewers assume that much on RTV is a performance and there is a growing recog- nition of the extent to which we all perform in real-life social interactions – a tendency that is only exacerbated by social media. But waiting for the mask to drop or for someone to reveal their true colors still appears to be a popular viewing pleasure (J. Jones

2003; Andrejevic 2004; Hill 2005; Skeggs and Wood 2009). Some participants appear to be more real or authentic than others, so we could recognize a scale of authenticity within performance (Kavka 2012: 94). When viewers want subjects to be "real" and to "keep it real," it is in the sense of behaving on screen like they behave in real life – but, of course, since most viewers don't know the participants off screen they have to speculate about what they would consider authentic or what authentic looks like on a TV show. There are also some paradoxes: if participants are amateur actors and inept at following a rough script, then they can either seem more real because not polished actors or less authentic because trying to act. Another seeming paradox is when participants insist that performing on screen leads to a more authentic sense of self, as Andrejevic (2004) and Kavka (2012) among others note. RTV subjects report that being on TV helps them "discover who they are." John Corner (2002) describes this process as "selving," where "true selves" emerge from "performed selves."

Producers, we know, are fond of creating extreme conditions and strong melodrama. But just because an emotion is induced or manipulated or strong doesn't necessarily mean it is fake. Inducement and exaggeration may also reveal deeper psychological truths; or they may not. Audience studies suggest that within RTV's *affective reality*, viewers react emotionally because real people are expressing real emotions and it is the emotion that creates the sense of authenticity (Kavka 2008; Sender 2012; Wood and Skeggs 2012).[15] It doesn't matter if the same viewers see much of the set-up as artificial: they invest in the participants' emotional realism and generally disapprove of false or deceptive expression. Of course, people often forget to compare on-screen strategizing with the exigencies of real life and so RTV may be realistic also when it exposes the almost unavoidable deceptions of everyday life. Gamedocs in particular encourage a good deal of deception and neither players nor viewers are quite settled on how to judge this performance. Many in both camps acknowledge the need for strategy but nevertheless expect minimum deception. Or viewers oscillate or occupy contradictory viewing positions, valuing both player truth and deception (Kavka 2012: 94). Periodically there is the discovery of egregious producer manipulation and then viewer websites are afire with discussions about how unreal reality TV is. Hence it may be that the most interesting relationship is between the participant, the camera, and *the viewer*, rather than inter-cast dynamics – except as they, too, are being affected by their appearance on TV. Viewers collaborate online when playing detective and exposing the cast or producers, dredging up pre-cosmetic surgery photos or evidence of digital editing. Indeed, this question of editing and authenticity seems more interesting to some viewers than the content of the drama. Producers are partly gratified by this level of engagement but also have to guard against it.

The attraction of the real

Some scholars have suggested that factual entertainment addresses a reality deficit, that it represents a longing for the real in the age of the virtual and digital, "a euphoric effort to reclaim . . . a sense of being in contact with the world by way of indexicality," given that digital images do not link in this way to actual referents (Fetveit 1999; see also Baudrillard 1993 [1990]; Dovey 2000; Andrejevic 2004). Daniel Boorstin saw a similar craving mid-century when he described Americans' "desperate hunger for the spontaneous, for the non-pseudo-event" in the form of crime stories and sports (1992 [1961]: 254), a fetishization of the real that is also taken up by Glynn (2000: 49–50). In this view, reality is an increasingly scarce resource in a world where both digital recording and impression management seem ever more prevalent. But, while it draws on the real, one can argue that RTV is contributing to its scarcity, turning more of raw experience into a commodified media product and overlaying lived experience with yet more TV grammar. After watching *Survivor*, people may begin to see their own co-workers as players in such a game, or others may feel they or their homes look like the "Before" images on makeover shows. (Two men allegedly tried to use this overlay to their advantage by telling pizza shop employees they were robbing that they were on a reality show called *You Just Got Robbed*.[16]) Cultural theorists such as Baudrillard and before him Boorstin have articulated the anxiety that everyday mediation may be causing a larger de-realization or loss of reality. According to this model, the media's mass production of symbols saturates the everyday with images of desire that serve to mask real sociopolitical relations.

Another theory is that RTV attracts viewers because it is voyeuristic and produces the same frisson of observing something amateur, intimate, and spontaneous. However, reality TV clearly departs from classic voyeurism in that the subjects know they are being watched and in any case audience surveys do not bear out the idea that voyeurism is a major attraction, or at least not in reported responses (e.g., Papacharissi and Mendelson 2007). Perhaps the viewer position is closer to pornography: paying to see the conscious performance of something usually private and intimate and doing so remotely and without any accountability. Baudrillard, who was one of the first major theorists to understand the novelty and significance of reality television (1983), declared RTV to be pornographic "because it is forced, exaggerated" (1988 [1987]: 21), and, of course, it often involves agreeing to exposure for money.

Reality TV and documentary

Reality TV's relation to documentary is a special concern of some scholars in Britain where there has been, and still is, a strong documentary tradition and misgivings about RTV's possible distortion or dilution of this tradition.[17] RTV can be seen as the outcome of broader trends such as a commercial push toward infotainment, a reduction of serious news gathering, and a general weakening of public service broadcasting: all the result of deregulation and privatization. RTV reflects a contemporary cultural transformation that privileges subjective, intimate, and emotional experience and this, it is argued, is having the effect of making documentary also more emotional, more confessional, and self-reflexive (e.g., Biressi and Nunn 2005). It could be argued that RTV also underlines some of the contrivances, subjectivities, and maybe even pretensions of traditional documentary. One could regard RTV as reme-diating documentary: adopting its techniques but making their use self-conscious, revealing the limits and manipulation in docu-mentary's "creative treatment of actuality" (John Grierson, circa 1926).[18] More neutrally, John Corner's influential essay (2002) on a post-documentary television culture points to new direc-tions in production and reception, but in an expansion or reloca-tion of documentary rather than its demise (p. 266). Noting how documentary energies have recently taken on additional functions such as play, performativity, and personalization (p. 264), Corner regards RTV as a new "diversion" in both senses (direction and entertainment), and not just failed documentary. Rather than framing RTV as a fall from a purer pre-lapsarian documentary into a more sensationalist, less socially worthy, and uninformative light entertainment, Corner's essay suggests that the comparison is invidious if they each have different aims (see also Bignell 2005: 19).

Theatrum mundi

Corner insists that the self-conscious performance on RTV is distinct from the routinized performance in everyday life such as Erving Goffman (1959) referred to (Corner 2009: 62). So one could argue that RTV problematizes the idea of performance and its elements of both expression (associated with the genuine) and display (associated with the fake). Judging by online posts, some viewers believe there is such a thing as a genuine self and that this can be witnessed on these programs. Others see reflected in RTV the assertion that there is no such thing as a stable, genuine self beyond the performance of identity (e.g., Kavka 2012: 92). The induced and acceptable level of performance may be format-dependent. Clearly gamedocs make strong demands for strategic performances and impression management, so players have to be simply *convincingly real* or authentic. Although, even here, many viewers still favor those who are not deceptive and they disappoint producers by not voting out the genuine-but-bland. In docusoaps, there is some displeasure when it is revealed that subjects are not what they seem. Typical revelations are that participants used to be strippers, have criminal records (usually financial fraud), or are just not as wealthy as they pretend to be. Sometimes assessing to what degree participants are authentically portraying themselves or are being authentically portrayed by others is the premise and theme of the show: for example, testing if one person really loves another or just pretends to do so in order to win some prize. Alternatively, it may be that those who are used to professional acting are playing the role of the ordinary or real person because, as Mark Andrejevic points out, this is currently a popular role to play (Andrejevic 2004: 10).

Extra-ordinary

What has become clear by now is that RTV is actually not much interested in reality if this refers to the mundane round of grocery shopping, cubicle work, and watching television. Instead it focuses on the extra-ordinary: on the ordinary person displaying extreme behavior because of an unusual situation, stress, or fantasy. Most RTV starts with one of the most extra-ordinary things that can happen to the ordinary – and the desire of many categorized as ordinary – which is to be televised. So both the participants' ordinariness and their different status from the ordinary are significant. RTV focuses on the deviant or unusually extrovert, the extreme everyday, the taboo. Intimate bodily functions and talk about sex and sexual display regularly appear on screen, although actual intercourse is rare and if depicted is usually blurred, in infrared, and under bedcovers. Naked bodies (with blurred and still "private" parts) do, however, appear on recent shows with titles like *Dating Naked* (VH1 2014) and *Buying Naked* (real estate) (TLC 2013–), not to mention work footage from *Gigolos* (Showtime 2011–). On the other hand, RTV also purports to show the ordinariness of seemingly extra-ordinary figures such as celebrities or exotic subgroups (more later).

Reality TV and real life: three phases

Reality TV draws our attention to, and at the same time ampli-
fies, the fact that our experience of reality is already mediated to
varying degrees and that media representations are part of our
experience of real life. To the extent that even basic sensory perception is a form of interpretation then all of our experience has
always been mediated and with the ongoing process of what we
might call *technological absorption* – whereby media technologies
are becoming more and more intimate and physically integrated
with us (Google glass, Apple Watch, implanted chips) – the ultimate medium will again be the human body. But, whether using
internal or external devices, it is that those who produce media
content interpret and represent our world to us that is our concern
here. RTV capitalizes on the still remaining distinction between
unfilmed and filmed experience. To date, I believe we have witnessed three major development phases in reality TV's relation
to real life. These have emerged in roughly chronological order
although they are today running concurrently, with some recent
variations. I mark each phase according to the relation between
filmed events and the process of filming. Each model has elements
of the others, but there are waves when one type of relationship
between viewer, participant, and producer becomes more central.

The first phase is programming that presents us with *an edited
reality in the observational mode*. Events are filmed as they unfold
and are then edited for broadcast; for example, *An American
Family* (PBS 1973), *The Family* (BBC 1974), *Cops* (Fox 1989–),
Sylvania Waters (ABC Australia 1992, BBC 1993). These can
be on-the-fly rough footage or quite slick productions, but they
still capture what is supposedly simply unfolding in real life. In
the 1990s the US market tended to go in the direction of *Cops*,
while the UK preferred docusoaps like *Airport*. In both scenarios
cameras go into an already extant physical and social environment and follow people as they go about their day – although
similar rescue shows and *America's Most Wanted* used reconstructions and actors because events happened before cameras

were involved. While interpersonal conflict usually erupts at some point and is obviously a focal point, the cameras also follow the day-to-day exigencies of people's lives without scripting events. This continues in shows like *Teen Mom* but in recent variations producers like to document more abnormal pre-existing situations such as pageants, polygamy, or pathological behavior. These are observational but heavily edited shows, unlike the recent "slow TV" of Scandinavia showing uncut hours and hours of train rides or swimming salmon.

The second phase emerged at the close of the last century when there was a surge in more managed and proactive models with *contrived settings and preplanned activities.* This trend originated in *Candid Camera* and then *The Real World* (MTV, 1992–), but it accelerated with the gamedocs *Survivor* (2000–) and *Big Brother* (2000–). This phase also encompasses today's talent competitions and dating shows. In these instances, participants are filmed in producer-created physical and social environments and events are scripted in a macro sense in order to produce drama; for example, a game structure guarantees a regular cycle of suspense and revelation, crisis and denouement. There are unpredictable votes but the order in which they are read or broadcast is determined for dramatic purposes. On competitive talent shows like *Top Chef* editors can influence judges' decisions, but this is acknowledged only in the fine print during the final credits and we do not know its extent. According to the US Communications Act of 1934, only contests of "intellectual knowledge, intellectual skill, or chance," may not be rigged, which presumably means that cooking, dancing, singing, or fashion design can. There was a crisis in Britain in the late 1990s when some fabrication and re-enactments were discovered both in documentaries and in docusoaps. Some scenes in the popular *Driving School* and elsewhere were apparently staged. The manipulation was minor but docusoaps lost some claim on the real and scholars have suggested that the more overt filming of a series like *Big Brother* was a response to this (e.g., J. Jones 2003; Holmes 2004a: 115; Ellis 2005). Again, its constructed transparency could be regarded as making it more authentic (Kavka 2012: 72–3).

In the third phase of reality TV, instead of constructing a set, producers *reach out into the actual world in order to transform it*. If the previous two phases were about surveillance, this phase includes making over what is surveilled. A broad and still strong category, this interventionist structure encompasses building, vehicle, or body makeovers, business turnarounds, therapeutic formats, and sex or parenting advice shows. Presumably a deep attraction of the makeover narrative is the primeval ordering of chaos, the transformation of ugliness into beauty, the emotional satisfaction of unmistakable improvement. It is not about the pleasure of masking but of appreciating and *admiring the mediation of the real*. The fact that the show affects what is being filmed is not a flaw to be minimized, rather the impact of the camera and what it brings are foregrounded and applauded because the show apparently benefits everyone involved – though producers still maintain the fourth wall and scrupulously avoid showing the filming. Mediation is in this sense thematized and we are given what Mark Andrejevic identifies as "access to the reality of mediation" as opposed to access to unmediated reality (2004: 214). Unlike the self-effacement of documentary and of fictional programming which succeed when the fact of mediation is hidden or forgotten, this transformative programming displays the benign power of TV to affect material and psychological reality. In fact, it mediates and makes over the world in the medium's own image, bringing more real life into TV culture and in line with its standards and conventions.

Recent trends

In today's programming we largely see the greater prominence of already nascent elements. As mentioned in the previous chapter, there is some more overtly "scripted reality." What is presented is akin to first-phase observation of people in their own environment but with more contrivance in terms of pre-planned dialogue and plot. These "softly" or "lightly" scripted series include *The Hills* and later *The Only Way Is Essex* (TOWIE) and *Made in*

Chelsea (E4 2011–). At the start of every episode of TOWIE is the disclaimer: "The tans you see might be fake but the people are all real although some of what they do has been set up purely for your entertainment." A producer acknowledges that the show is "stage-managed" reality which they approach like a live show with a detailed running order.[19] Field producers collaborate with participants, talking to them off camera and then planning scenes together that will tell their story. They don't feed the cast specific lines but they do set up who will speak to whom about what. Also referred to in the last chapter is an increase in self-reflexivity, particularly in long-running series like docusoaps whose casts are increasingly open about being on TV. These series are not reflexive because the camera is acknowledged but because they become about the effect of being on TV. On this level, the series is creating the reality it presents and is highlighting what elsewhere is more oblique, which is that much RTV is about *making television* and about the *impact of mediation on real life*.

Both self-reflexivity and a heavier scripting are highlighted in reunion shows. These offer something of a behind-the-scenes look at the process of making the TV show, to produce a different relation between participants, producers, and viewers. *The Real World* had its first reunion show in 1995 and then at the end of every season since 2000, but the impact of the reunion really took off with Bravo's *Real Housewives* programming (since 2006). Then there is the capitalization of viewership through the potentially infinite regress of viewers watching viewers watching TV. *Gogglebox* (C4 2013–) and *The People's Couch* (Bravo 2013–) film ordinary people watching TV shows that were broadcast during the previous week. The original show and viewer reactions to it are then folded into another form of RTV, making the viewing position also self-conscious and self-reflexive. Viewers-watching-viewers-watching-TV sounds contrived but as a representation of everyday life it may be a particularly authentic form of reality television: despite it being a big part of many people's lives, TV watching is not commonly depicted on TV.

Ordinary celebrity

To further understand the relation between this programming and real life, it is time to consider more closely the role of previously unmediated people who appear on screen: how they perform and how they are regarded by viewers and by themselves. News, documentary, talk shows, quiz shows, all have incorporated ordinary subjects for years – though, outside documentary, the attention has generally been limited and brief. Unprecedented is the prolonged and intimate access to the private lives of previously unmediated people for purely entertainment purposes and the extent to which this subject matter pervades the TV schedule. As a result, reality TV has now become an important part of the celebrity manufacture process, particularly of *ordinary* celebrity (e.g., Holmes 2004a) – a term with some of the same tension as "reality TV." Ordinary celebrities are generally famous simply because of media exposure. Their celebrity is undiluted or absolute in the sense that professional actors can talk about pride in their craft but RTV stars are more nakedly interested in just being famous or in using their fame to boost other careers. For some it may indeed be a matter of pride that they are famous just for being themselves. So instead of the already famous trading some intimate details, here we have *intimacy* that then *brings fame*.

Sometimes fame manufacture is the premise of the show (talent contests or career shows) and at other times a significant by-product. For producers, celebritization provides a cheap, in-house production of figures who can generate buzz for their own show or promote a future series. Indeed, some formats are explicitly about producing stars for the home channel, as in *Food Network Star* (2005–) or *HGTV Design Star* (2006–). As RTV evolves, we can see increased instances of re-circulation where characters from one RTV show cross-pollinate others. Some alumni seem pretty desperate to climb back in: for example, one back door for return to the limelight is to reveal your deepest failings in personal relationships on something like *Couples Therapy* (VH1 2012–). While celebrity is usually secondary for producers, the hope of acquiring this status is a strong draw for lowly paid and easily managed participants. The majority of these appear and disappear without trace, but still RTV feeds and intensifies a popular contemporary desire not just to know about celebrities but to *be* one. As more people report that what they most want in life is fame, reality TV is using its status as a mass medium to create this highly desirable commodity. It is TV showing off, in a way, as it heads into a future of convergence. Ordinary celebrity comes out of a new media environment where anyone can create a "following," but RTV demonstrates the extant power of its mass audience reach. The nature of RTV also means that viewers can imagine themselves on screen, so ordinariness creates empathy and affinity.

Reality TV self-reflexively showcases celebrity as a process and invites viewers to be part of the process. For some time, commentators have recognized the making and managing of celebrity as an "industry" (e.g., Gamson 1994; Marshall 1997), but RTV viewers have an opportunity to co-create the celebrity (by voting, blogging) and so feel engaged and even invested. Newly minted RTV celebrities have limited autonomy, their fame being largely the property of those professionals who manufactured it. This makes plain the fact that fame is a form of economic leverage and cultural currency. As Alison Hearn (2008) points out, fame has been considered a commodity in legal terms since 1953 when the "right to publicity" law was introduced. This law recognizes that a celebrity image can enhance the commercial values of commodities or services and so the public persona can be treated as a brand or saleable commodity in its own right. Indeed, stars have long been a key device for raising capital for media projects (Dyer 1986: 5). In RTV we get to see the apparatus of celebrity production in foregrounded strategies of marketing and promotion (Andrejevic 2004: 5), so celebrity creation is no longer a by-product (Kavka 2012: 146). Former stars also reappear as media zombies somewhat the worse for wear as they stumble around in a half-dead, half-alive state trying to reanimate their careers. Even when the TV appearance boosts or creates fame, much also depends on subsequent amplification in magazines and websites and these favor certain formats: for example, currently docusoap stars are a staple in celebrity magazines (*The Real Housewives*; *Kardashians*; *The Only Way Is Essex*).

What RTV most clearly illustrates is how celebrity can be a result of sheer media exposure with or without any definable talent other than attracting attention, resulting in what Chris Rojek (2001) has dubbed "celetoids." This acquiring of celebrity without any need for training, credentials, or talent Laura Grindstaff (2011a) refers to as "self-service television," where ordinary people can help themselves to a celebrity persona (p. 45). RTV is clearly a prime site for producing the kind of tautological famous-for-being-famous status predicted by Boorstin. Indeed, in some instances lack of talent is the point: for producers can make money by inviting audiences to laugh at its absence. In addition, RTV notoriously throws people up to the surface of culture who possess not just a deficit of talent but also of moral character. So in many instances people don't collectively look up to RTV celebrities so much as down on them. Frequently viewers feel toward RTV personalities, "a pleasurable blend of contempt, envy, skepticism and prurience" (Tyler and Bennett 2010: 375). This consolidates a modern separation between fame and admiration.

Few RTV alumni have made it big in Hollywood (one being Jennifer Hudson), but talent formats have created some successful recording stars, from Kelly Clarkson to Susan Boyle. Some others go on to find work in advertising or TV, although they are more likely to re-appear within RTV circuits. Reality celebrities don't usually compete with major stars, but they *have* inevitably reduced opportunities for professional actors. Sue Collins (2008) describes RTV as producing "dispensable celebrity," that is, low-capital audience attractors whom broadcasters can use, re-use, and also drop with relative ease. Not as often remarked upon is that RTV also illustrates the wider impact of the idea of celebrity throughout the economy. Its programming intensifies the celebritization of previously less marked positions and it buttresses the popular notion that fame is a signal of professional success in many walks of life, from realtors to surgeons. In this capacity, the creation of celebrity provides a rapid illustration of the rewards of neoliberal capitalism: i.e., individual success through self-promotion. Not all RTV participants seek fame, however. Many temporarily give up privacy in order to earn help of some kind and happily return to anonymity immediately after: indeed many makeover subjects regard being normal or ordinary as an achievement. Nevertheless, seeing other people's desperation, witnessing what they will put up with for a chance at fame, reinforces how important it is to be visible and recognized in today's expanding attention economy.

Conclusion

So far we have seen that reality TV generally encompasses elements that are spontaneous or raw, and in that sense "real," and other elements that are staged or contrived, and therefore less real though still actual. All of RTV is characterized by this combination of staged actuality but its various formats construct different relationships to real life depending on popular trends or target audience. Most viewers recognize the mediation of experience that is taking place: they enjoy looking for the unmasked moment and they enjoy identifying and critiquing the contrivance. If RTV highlights the performances of everyday life, the fact that mediation can so transform and validate ordinary people is a testament, finally, to the medium's power.

3

Social Television: Reality TV and New Media

Reality TV is particularly useful for underlining some of the opportunities and challenges television faces in an increasingly convergent environment. Its modern form was born in an attempt to maximize multiplatform engagement, and it continues to provide examples of social television in the form of interlocking broadcast and internet use. Computers and other mobile devices are today re-contextualizing television: that is, they are "changing what it is that television can do, for whom it can do it, and under what conditions" (Turner and Tay 2009: 3). One way of looking at RTV is as *TV's version of the internet*, capitalizing as it does on the net's culture of ordinary participation and public revelation, whether actors are direct participants or peripheral interactors. What reality TV highlights is the distant closeness, the superficial intimacy of mediated sociality, whether on TV or online.

Yet in many respects TV–web interactions remain underdeveloped. Since they are locked into a linear temporal sequence (with high costs per minute), TV broadcasters could use the internet's infinite spatialization to present extra material, but to date this has been largely underutilized. Public broadcasters like the BBC and PBS have been more inclined to explore this opportunity, usually in the form of further educational material whose links are publicized during the broadcast, but commercial producers are mostly content to invite viewers to tweet or shop and, since the live *Big Brother* webcasting at the dawn of RTV, have shown little interest in providing extra footage. I observed some deeper forms of

TV–web interactivity over a decade ago (Deery 2003) but since then have seen less synchronous interweaving than one might have expected.[1] Today, most official websites merely show past clips or future teasers and do little to connect first and second screens as a simultaneous experience, though this coactivity is slowly being driven by viewers.[2]

A strong attraction for RTV viewers is being able to analyze and discuss episodes amongst themselves during or after the broadcast, on laptops, tablets, or other mobile devices. Pushing through the broadcast threshold, they coactively *articulate* distinct media in different combinations – using articulation in Stuart Hall's sense of joined but distinct. This practice complicates and enriches the relations between participants, viewers, and producers in ways illustrated earlier but examined more closely here. What is clear is that the drama now extends beyond the show. Combined media use creates richer, denser, and stickier relationships between participants and viewers that have already begun to destabilize concepts such as "audience," "text," and even "television." Products evolve into *processes* and texts into *texting* in the sense of open and open-ended material (Deery 2012: 34–5). Hence, as Su Holmes (2004b) and others observe, it is becoming less evident where media scholars should draw the line between text and reception.

Scholars who have examined RTV and the internet consider how cross-platform use has affected production, distribution, and reception (e.g., Tincknell and Raghuram 2002; Deery 2003, 2012; Andrejevic 2004, 2011; Holmes 2004b; S. Ross 2008; Gillan 2011; Edwards 2013). As we might expect, there are different repercussions for different constituencies and while some studies celebrate how viewers and participants are being empowered, there are advantages for producers and broadcasters, too, as they establish new arrangements between power and profit. Because being able to demonstrate strong viewer interactivity now impresses advertisers when pitching shows, networks increasingly include not just Nielsen ratings but also Twitter mentions and website hits. In what follows, I will not be looking at every specific activity or affordance (some of these will have changed by the time this is published), but at how web use affects larger relations between viewers and programs, particularly as evidenced on reality TV. One striking development, I suggest, is that cross-media activities are re-contextualizing broadcast *space* and, crucially, *time*. Multiplatformicity makes accessible different and distinct timelines and, as media devices converge, narratives and identities buckle and fragment, sometimes to the disadvantage of producers and participants.

In order to clarify the economics and power differentials behind recent technological trends, I want to distinguish between the two often loosely conflated ideas of participation and interactivity. I use participation to refer to people appearing on TV broadcasts and interactivity to refer to the viewer's activities that engage with, but *do not directly affect*, the TV text. Subjects thus participate *in* or interact *with*, but in neither case is their power or influence great within the official broadcast or its industrial context (Deery 2012). (RTV is emphatically not "public access TV.") Interacting with the text is also fundamentally delimited. To interact *with* indicates distance between distinct objects and, while viewers might feel their input is participatory, it is usually more accurately described as a supplementary relationship with an already formed text. Even if we put the emphasis on what viewers do with the text, the distinction, the temporal priority, and much of the economics remain the same for the broadcast content. Traditionally, this text is fixed, meaning its content is presented in one form to a mass audience: it is not customized or individualized for individual viewers and is exactly reproducible whether on a TV monitor or elsewhere.

What has changed is reception, or what might be better called viewer engagement. Today, both viewers and participants can extend the broadcast material and continue creating multi-authored and open-ended texts. Moreover, mobile devices mean audience engagement is ever more integrated into everyday life. Typically, this activity springs from an original broadcast text that all share, although occasionally people join online conversations who apparently haven't watched the TV program or at least the episode being discussed. The point is that the potential for cross-media viewing now shapes TV reception even if an individual viewer doesn't watch anything other than the broadcast show. Viewers may choose to have different experiences of the TV text and, whether or not they themselves publicly interact with the show (e.g., posting online comments), all viewers can now witness more forms of interaction: interaction between viewers, between viewers and participants, and between participants and other participants online. Some of these interactions may subsequently and indirectly affect future broadcasts or reception of these texts, so interactivity can become participatory in future texts. Having the internet available, even as a potential, may also affect in an anticipatory fashion the viewer's experience of the TV broadcast. If, as I watch, I know that I or others will be commenting on the broadcast, then I will view with this in mind and possibly under the influence of prior viewer comments. This means that the self-consciousness of TV performers is being matched by the self-consciousness of their viewers.

The producer's role

TV and other media devices can be rivals or mutual enhancements. Usually they are both. Online interactivity can play an important role in sustaining viewer interest and building loyalty to a show or even channel, so important in an age of surfing and time shifting. If even negative commentary leads to a bigger and more engaged audience whose reactions can be circulated inexpensively online, then broadcasters have little to lose by encouraging such user-generated meta-discourse. By letting go of some control, they add value to the primary media property – not least because claiming to be more open and democratic, or at least accessible, is good PR for television, especially among the all-important younger demographic. Online activity and fan autonomy may also add authenticity to a TV show – although online interaction is not guaranteed to be authentic.[3] As many commentators have under-lined, but most especially Mark Andrejevic, online technologies allow others to extract commodifiable information about TV viewers and conduct economic surveillance. What is ordinarily the viewer's private activity becomes traceable and monetized and so viewers perform the "work of being watched," turning their leisure time into something that can be monitored, repackaged, and sold (Andrejevic 2004: 36). This reflects the broader contemporary blurring of "work" and "life" due to a combination of high productivity demands and mobile technologies. In addition, the extension of cast relationships into personal blogs or tweets means that the distinction between private and public has come under even more stress and is difficult to define in both spatial and temporal terms, for both TV participant and viewer.

Another configuration is what Bravo calls the "social edition" of shows, in which not terribly insightful tweets from viewers or participants are displayed on a scroller during a repeat airing. This overlay allows broadcasters to enhance the profitability of previous material now billed as "new" again. Presumably they hope some viewers will watch again to see if their comments were selected or are just curious about what others think. Sometimes viewers are invited to send text messages during a live broadcast, as with *Big Brother* on E4. This input doesn't usually affect TV participants but does appear on the broadcast and so is a form of supplementary participation. In the other direction, producers have also sent text messages to viewers alerting them about events on an upcoming broadcast. The British broadcasting of *Big Brother* has, in fact, led the way in this kind of interactive digital TV (Bignell 2005: 157).

On both sides of the Atlantic, producers manage and exploit as far as possible the paratext of the internet, but a labor dispute is mounting about whether TV production staff should get paid extra for working on a website or blog. There is a problem of classification in some instances, for online activities might be categorized as advertising or promotion rather than regular editorial material. Cast members are also often obliged to produce a regular blog, commenting on their show or other shows in the broadcaster's repertoire. Some series extend their effect on viewers in the form of online advice or instruction, sometimes for a fee: for example, weight loss shows like *The Biggest Loser* (Sender 2012: 42–3). Theoretically this could be an important prosocial venture, but in actuality little practical information is posted on RTV sites and broadcasters appear more interested in simply merchandising information (as DVDs and books). Perhaps some general social knowledge can be gleaned from watching RTV, but surveys suggest viewers don't value it for its pragmatic information (Andrejevic 2004: 124; Hill 2007). Skeggs and Wood (2012) found that viewers report learning little and in fact take pleasure in critiquing expert advice. Perhaps RTV instruction is therefore best understood as pleasurably *vicarious and hypothetical* ("If I were to decorate my house, I would. . .").

Viewer activity

Judging the performance of others is a big part of watching RTV, and not just on talent or competition shows. On online forums hoards of anonymous, invisible others weigh in on the minutiae of other people's lives. This platform encourages appointment viewing because viewers wish to discuss an episode with others during or immediately after its initial broadcast. Internet use, in other words, can re-invigorate traditional features of the mass medium, including the notion that a television program is a synchronous event for large numbers of viewers.[4]

RTV illustrates well how TV shows don't have to be admired or approved of in order to be watched. Viewers can be invested though alienated, avid though hostile. One study found that negative emotions regarding a show were a stronger motivator for engaging in online discussion than a positive attitude (Godlewski and Perse 2010: 165–6). Hostile tweets or bloggers' recaps become another form of entertainment with their own fans. Recappers summarize and analyze each episode, typically in a witty and sarcastic fashion, and some responders say this online commentary motivates them to watch the broadcasts. Online forums encourage viewers to be productive, to make the show interesting for themselves while at the same time providing feedback to producers (Andrejevic 2008).

Much viewer interaction can be characterized as gossip, meaning an informal exchange about the personal lives of mutually known (and real) persons. This interchange could be regarded as compensating for the anonymity of contemporary society and as answering a nostalgic desire for community life, or an image of a previous life (Biressi and Nunn 2005: 107; Andrejevic 2014). Certainly RTV viewer interactivity is typically experiential and more about sharing an experience than divulging information. Users write as though about a personal acquaintance or friend, some directly addressing RTV cast members and offering advice, support, or censure that is meant to impact them beyond their television appearance. Others coach and strategize about their TV role.

Some viewers mine the internet to locate material that subverts cast roles or histories. Displaying an impressive collective intelligence, they gleefully hunt down proof of lying or unearth unsavory information, court documents, mug shots. A similarly indirect effect can be felt in gamedocs, but in this case the interaction is a cat-and-mouse game between producers and viewers. As Henry Jenkins (2006) and others have noted, in order to preserve their primary selling point (the winner's identity), producers edit material both on television and online in order to throw viewers off the scent. Though apparently amicable, this interaction is at base antagonistic and constitutes a move to protect profitability: hence producers have sued viewers who run spoilers (*Survivor*; *The Bachelor*). Some viewers organized online to fly banners over the first US *Big Brother* site to try to affect the game in a form of "narrative activism" or culture jamming (Wilson 2004: 324), and another fan/sleuth claimed he found the secret *Survivor* site and from a helicopter dropped chocolates to its hungry participants below, much to the producers' annoyance (Deery 2003: 173).

The main form of invited mass participation is audience voting. This can affect an ongoing series either as a central mechanism, a limited determinant of one program segment, or because it gives rise to an on-air prize or announcement, such as the viewers' favorite cast member. As an aggregation of many individuals' input, voting is a valuable commodity that can't be exploited by others; in fact, producers guard as private property any information regarding how many votes were cast and for whom. Audience voting goes back to the earliest forms of TV: *The Original Amateur Hour* (1948) invited viewers to vote via telephone or postcard; *Opportunity Knocks* (Thames 1956–78) was proud of its instant audience "clapometer"; and viewers of *You Asked For It* (DuMont, ABC 1950–9) mailed in requests for celebrity appearances or other content. Today, participatory voting is still comparatively rare but certainly useful for building viewer loyalty: it made quite a splash with real-time voting on live broadcasts of *Rising Star* (ABC 2014–) and *The Singer Takes it All* (C4 2014–).

RTV demonstrates how a mass medium can generate income by selling back to audiences content created by audiences, with considerable profits not only for the TV industry but also other communication companies. In Britain, concerns were raised about the low odds of anyone winning phone-in competitions and the huge profits generated by alliances between broadcasters, producers, and phone companies. One parliamentary committee considered reclassifying vote-in reality shows as a form of gambling and official investigations and fines occurred after various "phone-in scandals." The regulator Ofcom fined broadcaster GMTV (now defunct) and its telecom ally for reaping profits from callers who had no chance of winning a competition. Other deceptive practices tarnished even the BBC, as when viewers thought their calls were affecting a live show that was actually pre-recorded (e.g., *Saturday Kitchen Live*, BBC1 2002–). That is, interactivity was presented as participation.

In interactive voting, audiences are encouraged to vote or indicate how they feel about a show without affecting broadcast content – and, again, this information typically doubles as market research. Some viewers seize more agency and leverage the internet in an antagonistic fashion. They organize boycotts of broadcasters or their advertisers in protest at the poor quality or degrading nature of the program content, the choice of particular cast members, the exploitation of subjects, or crass commercialization. It is, of course, difficult to judge if such people do boycott or affect ratings, but there have been a few striking instances. In 2009, a few viewers organized a boycott of the winning single from Britain's *The X Factor* (ITV 2004–) and encouraged people to buy instead a 1992 song by the left-wing, anti-corporate Rage Against the Machine. This recording did outsell the X *Factor* winner, though only by a small margin. Viewers have also periodically organized an *American Idol* "vote-for-the-worst" campaign to promote mediocre singers and thereby subvert the show's claim of discovering real talent (using viewers as unpaid focus groups). But so far none of this activity has scuttled TV productions and often profits telecom companies. As has for some time been recognized, the basic broadcast model is that viewers constitute a largely passive labor force commodified in the form of ratings (Smythe 1981; Jhally 1990). They also contribute financially by buying equipment, paying content providers (cable, satellite), electricity providers, etc. However, this is not a zero-sum arrangement. Today, viewers increasingly produce their own material that others can capitalize on, but this doesn't mean they can't benefit from this process. That viewers' labor can be exploited by others doesn't preclude it having real value for them also, offering as it does the potential for sociability, self-expression, collective action, and creativity.

Temporal dislocations

What is striking, today, is how the use of other platforms has complicated the TV narrative in temporal terms. There are generally at least two distinct timelines. One timeline is that of broadcast schedule, the episode-by-episode revelations of previously filmed and edited material (with typically about six months between filming and broadcast). Another is the ongoing timeline of cast members as they continue to live out their lives between series, communicating with the public right up to the present moment if they choose (e.g., tweets). This *persistence of vision*, the existence of participants beyond the broadcast event, may compromise the more homogeneous and stable TV text. Magazine or online updates can and do preempt the narrative of an upcoming TV series and so spoil its marketable suspense. The more popular the reality show and the more people want to read about its cast, the more this fame takes away from the upcoming broadcast series, so the shows become a victim of their own success. New input may also retrospectively alter the interpretation of a past season. Some retrospection or anticipation is managed by producers, but much else is anarchic and complicates not only the series' temporal sequence but also whose reality it is, meaning which version of reality is accepted. Real-time updates take away some of the authenticity of the broadcast or its sense of immediacy at the very least. Producers can try to prevent leakage where they can, but this is often futile. For example, one *Top Chef* producer tried unsuccessfully to stop diners tweeting that they saw the show's hosts in a New Orleans restaurant, thus spoiling the suspense of the next location. He apparently forgot that his management of TV participants did not extend to real-life events and that he had no right to order private individuals to cease communicating.

Occasionally the participants' reaction to popular press coverage is folded into the broadcast. This is not new – *The Family* (1974) was aired only four weeks after filming and participants were able to incorporate public reactions to them while filming the show (Holmes 2008; Kavka 2012: 36). On today's docusoaps, by the time a topic is broadcast it may have been preempted by tabloid coverage so the real-ness of the show – the fact it involves real people who can feature in other media – also makes the TV broadcast more obviously constructed, since viewers can't think of the drama depicted within the series as being *in their present*. The short-circuiting of different timelines reminds viewers that turning real life into television is a process and that it takes time. Alternatively, when what the press or viewers uncover is not shared on the TV show, this reinforces the extent to which participants are performing roles and not necessarily being candid. Indeed, Su Holmes notes that tabloid and press coverage sometimes sell their disclosures as a deeper authenticity (2004a: 123). *The Only Way Is Essex* is unusual for reducing the gap between event and broadcast to three days, so it quickly incorporates cast reactions to viewer comments and to previous broadcast episodes. TOWIE producers – who claim the show is about the interaction between "transmission, fame and being in the moment" – update viewers daily on Twitter and Facebook about the cast members' lives.⁵ If there is too much of a lag between broadcasts and social media talk, the narrative becomes too confusing, producers maintain. All of which suggests that social media may force TV broadcasters to change their production practices. A similar US experiment called *The Singles Project* (Bravo 2014) broadcasts dating encounters that took place in the week prior and, both during the broadcast and between broadcasts, viewers are invited to provide feedback to participants via social media, offering dating advice or casting suggestions. The on-screen participants are unusually open about being on a TV show and about receiving viewer feedback and this quickly edited format largely avoids the asynchronicity and real-life spoilers that plague other docusoaps.

Multiple perspectives

One main consequence of internet use is the underscoring of differences between cast and viewer perspectives. The dominant thematic content of many docusoaps is the disputing of truth and the dramatic irony that erupts when there are gaps in awareness and viewing access among participants, effects which are sometimes highlighted by editors. Viewers are able to contrast the players' behavior toward fellow participants and their behavior when alone in the confessional mode. Obviously they may be acting the whole time, but it is remarkable how often they seem to open up and feel comfortable with this kind of revelation: especially in game situations, the confession to camera may be a cathartic release from the strategizing elsewhere. Outside game formats, it is curious how often participants reveal more to the TV camera than to those in their real-life inner circle – in this sense, then, RTV becomes a form of public privacy. Participants frequently say things behind each other's backs and then deny having said it, apparently forgetting about the recording that is quietly subverting their claims and that they may be forced to witness later. They perversely forget, or choose to ignore, the medium's function, which is to record actions for public consumption. Drama is therefore generated because of the difference between technological and human memory (precise record and subjective recollection) and because of a temporal and experiential gap between filming and broadcasting.

One of the challenges for participants is that, not having a prior and mutually shared script, they don't know in advance how they will be portrayed after final editing and as episodes air they become first-time viewers, or what we might call *participant-viewers*, of an edited version of their lives (most receive DVDs only a few days ahead of the broadcast). Producers capitalize on this release by encouraging cast members to produce a regular blog in which they comment on each episode as it airs. They write about what it is like to view a TV episode and be a viewer of their own lives. This opens up new veins of drama and conflict due to a collision of different levels of insight and viewing access: people now know what others said behind their back both on television and online. Time lapse plays real havoc with the people involved and opens old wounds, including life-long primary relationships within families. Individuals may be working towards reconciliation but the broadcast leads to outbreaks of renewed hurt and hostility. This is not how most of us go through life and when they are pushed together physically and apart emotionally, few relationships survive the public scrutiny. As the series continue, they spiral inevitably into more and more hurt and alienation, providing the requisite humiliation quotient and inspiring gleeful online invective. It is fair to say that RTV participants are subject to more criticism and more public criticism than people might ordinarily expect in everyday life and, given that these participants are not playing fictional roles, comments about their TV performance can produce very real emotions that are carried into their everyday lives, and therefore into future TV broadcasts.

We might at first dismiss this lopsided interchange of viewer and cast member as a pseudo-intimacy, as a delusion on the viewer's part, but given their posts' impact on TV participants it may be a new form of real, albeit highly mediated, intimacy that at least in some regards constitutes a mutual relationship beyond the pronounced asymmetry of the parasocial. One of the main talking points in online posts, and one reason why viewers feel their input is necessary, is the awareness gap due to technically and socially limited perception. A good example is the *Real Housewives* franchise whose casts appear to possess little understanding of the impact or nature of their own behavior, despite – or because of – their focus on themselves. Viewers' posts appear to enjoy puncturing their delusions, a reaction quite different from criticizing a fictional character who would not be insulted, or even *there* to react in any way. A viewer might congratulate an author for producing a convincingly obtuse character, but viewers don't congratulate a person for being obtuse, even if this enhances the drama, unless in a highly sarcastic and barbed manner. The dramatic irony that so often erupts on these docusoaps – at times highlighted by flashbacks inserted by editors – carries with it a moral charge that encourages emphatic and self-righteous correction from viewers and others. The ability to use one medium to undercut another appears to be a considerable attraction. Drama comes from a tension between what the viewers see, what the participants see, what the viewers think the participants should see, and even what the participants think the viewers should see.

RTV commentary illustrates well the internet's asymmetry, its lack of accountability and reciprocity. That viewer vitriol is widespread and aggressive is, no doubt, in part a function of the medium's anonymity. But its targets are not anonymous and when cast members complain about having their feelings hurt, discussions arise online about the etiquette and parameters of online communication. Some viewers insist on maintaining the same civility that one would expect in a face-to-face encounter. Others reject this as anachronistic and maintain that expectations about privacy and personal honor have to shift when someone signs on for a reality show. Clearly, as the media continue to converge and broadcasts continue to employ real people, the power and entitlements of various agents are still being negotiated.

Because cast members are real people having real experiences and making real decisions, viewers feel able to critique and make moral judgments about them as responsible agents. This response raises intriguing, and mostly unanswerable, questions such as: Are we less tolerant of *real* than *fictional* characters? Are we quicker to make and communicate moral judgments about real characters because they may read our comments and therefore be reformed, or at least deservedly chastised? If we "know" reality figures it is in a publicly intimate way whose mediation perhaps encourages severity; for seeing people as images on a screen may make them objects it is convenient and acceptable to dismiss and ridicule. Cast members don't usually acknowledge reading viewer posts or being affected by them, except sometimes obliquely on reunion shows and in their own blogs. They often express hurt or anger, but they may be just as concerned about how criticism affects their brand and future on the show. Viewers' online comments are also monitored by producers and may determine who is offered a con-tract renewal, again affecting present and future programming. It is unlikely that producers care how negative the attention is, but participants *do* care and many mount defenses by constructing a more flattering, orthodox interpretation of their TV role online, apparently some with the help of professional publicity agents. Increasing numbers also use Facebook and Twitter as well as print magazines to present their side of the various fights they get into and so continue the drama there. Many use the convention that blogs are confessional and non-fictional to try to counteract their image on professionally managed mass broadcasts – though of course there is nothing about the form of a blog that precludes it being deceptive, managed, or indeed fictional. Some cast members have pretended to be viewers in order to mount a stealth defense: one *Real Housewives* participant is suspected of adopting multiple personae to defend herself in online viewer exchanges and using fake Amazon reviews to boost sales of her book. Needless to say, this deception and trespassing in *their* zone angers viewers, not least because it threatens to undermine the integrity of the entire program – with its genuine viewer interaction – another reality that producers and participants are jointly selling to the public. When criticized, a defense that participants mount is the limited nature of the real on RTV; they retort that the viewers who criti-cize them don't actually know them and that the show doesn't tell the whole story. Nevertheless, some viewers characterize their criticism as a right and the cast member's responses as an expected engagement, reflecting what Tincknell and Raghuram (2002) identify as the audience's feeling of "ownership" when it comes to reality programming (p. 211). Viewers complain if participants stop blogging (perhaps out of hurt feelings). They assert that viewers are an important part of the economic circuit and that the participants' celebrity and income depends on them.

Reunion implosion

An interesting format that has received little critical attention is the reunion show when the cast of docusoaps or gamedocs are forced to publicly confront each other just after the regular series has been broadcast. In what has become part TV analysis and part day of reckoning, viewers are guaranteed a dramatic internal implosion as different levels of cast awareness collide. These two- or three-episode extensions, which are taped live and presented as an occasion, frequently attract higher ratings than the regular series. They typically make the most of being beyond the TV broadcast by drawing on online comments, magazine articles, and phone calls. This format also allows meta-critical references to the fact that the prior series was an edited TV production. Much conflict comes from critiquing how being on the show has affected cast members or examining their motives for participating, often provoked by interjected questions from viewers. By now players have a more comprehensive and often acrimonious view of events and the reunion therefore extends the dominant thematic content of much RTV, which boils down to who is telling the truth and who is "being real." It also gestures toward what might be called the ultimate theme of reality TV: *what it means to be mediated on television.*

Reunion shows involve lots of squirming, bitter fake laughter, bold-faced bravado, angry tears, and much disputing of facts. Producers generally allow different unsupported interpretations and counter-claims to co-exist. Even simple factual matters don't get resolved because producers rarely use the full evidentiary nature of the filmed archive. Of course there are some technical and economic difficulties in cuing material during a live recording, but it is also in the producers' interest to allow disputes to fester and thereby keep participants and viewers engaged. Online viewer commentary is not exactly face-to-face criticism, but it is not behind the subjects' backs either, so the exchange produces a particular form of discomfort. We get some insight into the impact of viewer feedback on reunion shows when participants openly discuss how well their stock has risen or fallen based on online comments, although they are often coy about the extent to which they read these posts. Occasionally, some vow that such feedback will make them alter their future behavior, whether it be parenting styles, marital relationships, or perhaps just how they behave on TV. So the recognition of audience is stronger here than on the filmed series: one exception being *The Salon* (C4 2003–4) where participants openly read online comments while still filming and incorporated viewer reactions into the television show (Holmes 2004b).

Another meta-critical format exploited by Bravo to promote its programming is the live talk show *Watch What Happens*, conjoining the earliest form of television, the live broadcast, with the latest online activity. There is some limited viewer-to-participant dialogue when host/RTV producer Andy Cohen incorporates viewer email, texts, tweets, and live phone calls and puts up live polls to assess the current popularity of his guests/employees, often putting two cast members head-to-head and so provoking further inter-participant drama. Of course, what all of these contributing viewers are doing (whether calling or tweeting) is supplying, free of charge, material that others sell for profit – as is spelled out in the fine print regarding such submissions.[6]

It is likely that TV broadcasts will increasingly feature online activity as a part of contemporary life; for example, currently *#RichKids of Beverly Hills* and *Online Dating Rituals of the American Male* (both Bravo 2014) feature people compulsively using laptops or smart phones and their texts or tweets are displayed on screen. Similarly, *The Secret Lives of Students* (C4 2014) extends surveillance into people's tweets, texts, phone calls,

Facebook entries, and Google searches. Viewers are watching people mediate their own lives through these devices – reflecting a practice that for many people is further decreasing the gap between mediation and real life. But TV can also deconstruct online interaction, as illustrated by *Catfish* (MTV 2012–) whose self-conscious aesthetics (cameras made visible on camera) trumps a rival medium when its visible, face-to-face, but still mobile mode of operation critiques internet anonymity.

Conclusion

Online extensions of TV broadcasts are becoming an increasingly vital component for all involved – producers, viewers, and participants – and the ontological, psychological, and commercial repercussions of this expansion require more analysis. Nick Couldry envisions mass media and interpersonal media continuing to intertwine in a sort of double helix (2011a: 197). Whatever shape it takes, clearly some new media features have already altered the television viewing experience, while others return to earlier models of viewership (appointment viewing, family/group experience). The problem for producers is knowing what kinds of viewers to address: those who watch only the TV broadcast, or those who also check out associated websites or press coverage. Different viewing experiences complicate what to edit and how to control the release of information. But while online activity may overflow the television text it does not wipe out its boundaries and, for economic reasons, the model of producing a fixed text for a large audience will likely remain in place for some time, even if individual viewers choose to watch the content at different times and places. To date, the television broadcast remains the originating text and the most common platform for making initial contact with the public. Over time this will likely change, as we see more original online broadcasts including those produced by distributers such as Netflix.

4

Advertising and Commercialization

This chapter will consider reality TV as a commercialized product and its role in consumerist cultures. There are two main issues here: (i) the manner in which this programming is produced and monetized, and (ii) how it represents consumer society and practices of consumption. I use *commercialization*, as opposed to commercialism, because the active verbal noun underlines process and agency: in this case, the turning of something into a commercial opportunity. We start with the premise that the ultimate motive behind most RTV, as with most other programming, is commercial profit. RTV came to prominence at a time when the television industry was coming under stress in an increasingly convergent and deregulated environment. When traditional economic models began to look fragile (high salaries, mass audiences, and high-priced spot ads), RTV producers looked for ways to redefine relations between audiences, advertisers, and delivery systems. In Europe, the spread of RTV signals for many the weakening of a public service tradition as publicly funded broadcasters increasingly come under pressure to compete commercially. In fact, RTV's growth has meant that *commercial and non-commercial programming more closely resemble each other*. Public service programming, the home of documentary and educational programming, has in many places become more consumption-oriented and sensationalized. It now imitates many of the practices of commercial competitors in order to justify the expenditure of public funds in a deregulated and often transnational market. At the same time, commercial channels can claim (with different degrees of credibility) to be producing instructional, educational, and even documentary programming. But while, generally speaking, if we want to understand how and why a media production occurred we need to "follow the money," this is not to say that there aren't other forces at play. It also says little about why viewers watch: producers often don't know this either.

What we can say is that RTV illustrates the media's role in an expanding service economy whose basic transaction is to *commodify experience*. Indeed, one of the most powerful effects of mediation is that it enables this kind of commercialization. RTV fulfills the basic formula of commercial broadcasting: by selling viewing access to TV participants, producers are also selling access to viewers, a product that is created in order to be sold to advertisers. Much RTV also displays and promotes consumption and so can be seen as reinforcing larger social trends such as the shift in advanced capitalism from an emphasis on manufacturing goods to manufacturing consumers.

Economics of production

RTV is not an amateur production. It is created and broadcast by paid professionals. But those who produce it have found some strategic ways to substantially reduce costs: for example, studies by Chad Raphael (2004) and Ted Magder (2009) detail how this is done. To begin with the monetization of content, reality shows have pioneered, reconditioned, or revived several forms of advertising: among them, product placement, sponsorship, designer ads (commercials made for a particular program), merchandising, and online brand extension. Given its early and aggressive adoption of these and other techniques, RTV once again offers a useful vantage point from which to gauge television's present and future economy.

On the production side, much (but not all) RTV programming is well known to be relatively cheap given that it often involves unpaid or non-unionized labor, modest sets or low-cost mobile filming with already extant settings and lighting, and the elimination of official writers and other professional staff.[1] Yet RTV programs often garner strong ratings: in fact, sometimes these are strong precisely because viewers like the seeming authenticity of a less polished product. Since the film-to-edit-to-broadcast time is short, imitations and spin-offs are easy to mount and successful formats are often adaptable for a global market. Broadcasters are able to purchase pre-packaged formats that require little further investment and promise advertisers proven results. Being high-concept, RTV formats often require only simple marketing in order to pique audience curiosity and, if ratings subsequently disappoint, not much time or money has been lost; producers can try the next concept or some legal variation thereof. RTV successes have loosened traditional season scheduling (with a summer downtime) and shows are now launched year-round. Reality formats are also eminently suited to today's narrowcasting to specialized audiences and, as we've seen, are often pioneering in monetizing cross-media use and interactivity.

Production staff

The production companies to which broadcasters allocate a particular series tend to employ independent contractors with limited benefits and little job security. Staff typically work long hours (including unpaid overtime) under intense working conditions and then, between series, have periods of no work at all (Hearn 2010). Reality TV is regarded as an entry-level job and most workers hope to graduate beyond this kind of production, though given its prominence finding jobs elsewhere is not easy. Even when line-by-line scripting is required (host patter or voiceovers), RTV producers reduce salaries by re-categorizing jobs from, say, writers to "story editors" or "segment producers." When the Writer's Guild of America (WGA) went on strike (2007–8), among their demands were that some RTV staff be accorded the status of writer with union pay and eligibility. These attempts have not succeeded and RTV continues to be invested in as a hedge against future strike action.[2] There is little industry incentive to do otherwise. Acknowledging a staff member as a writer would mean not only increasing their compensation but also admitting that much RTV is scripted.

It could be argued that the employment situation on RTV (on and off screen) reflects the precarious and flexible nature of post-Fordist labor relations that depend on rapid results, group tasking, and short-term contracts (Hearn 2010; also Bratich 2007, 2011). As is often noted, today's employment expectations often erase the distinction between paid work and unpaid leisure, a pattern illustrated both by subjects whose filmed leisure becomes work and by those filming them whose unpaid labor often dwarves their recompensed hours. For those behind the cameras, as with TV subjects, employers expect the *immaterial labor* that comes from drawing on one's personality, creating social networks, and being "always on," as is well illustrated by Laura Grindstaff's study of TV producers (2002) and Vicki Mayer's research on casting producers (2011b, 2014). These practices also resemble the conflation of work/leisure and the commodification of socializing and creativity in the online economy (e.g., Andrejevic 2011).

Participants

Reality TV enjoys a lucrative labor situation, wherein people beg to work for free or for modest salaries, or in hopes of winning prizes that represent a fraction of the broadcaster's profits.[3] Once engaged, they are bound to contracts very much to the advantage of others. For example, talent show contestants are locked into deals that primarily profit music labels and broadcasters: the latter can even get a cut of post-broadcast live tours. As Graeme Turner (2010: 15) points out, this is a form of vertical integration that controls how inexpensively minted stars are marketed before, during, and after production. The home grown variety is cost effective and can be recycled in other series or in "all-star" or celebrity shows. Only some cast members get to negotiate substantially after a series proves successful, but producers discipline even these by not necessarily renewing everyone and at the same time generating publicity as they make casting decisions for an upcoming season. Gamedocs' iron-clad contracts focus on not disclosing winners and losers since these suspenseful elements are a key selling point. Most RTV producers aim to secure participant novelty value by making applicants confirm they have not previously appeared on other shows and by restricting future work opportunities. While being filmed, participants must remain commercially pure by not wearing brand labels on or off the show, unless those of official sponsors, and they must be available at any time to advertise the series. All this is different from the participation of documentary subjects who are not usually paid and don't typically seek TV coverage for their own financial gain.

Investigations are just beginning into the labor status of RTV participants and the extent to which they might be subject to the same legal rights, protections, and compensation as other workers. In 2005, a court ruling in France determined that participants in some reality formats are indeed subject to existing labor laws (Dauncey 2010: 316; Jost 2011; Andrejevic 2011). One legal argument is that, like most jobs, RTV involves subordination to an employer and the execution of tasks under this authority (Jost 2011: 36). Some cast members now earn salaries that rival professional actors and official "talent" like hosts or judges are paid professional rates; on some shows it seems even audience members are paid (Benza 2005: 107). Still many RTV formats depend on not paying participants much at all and imposing difficult working conditions: there are often restrictions on movement and experience (media blackout, isolation from family and friends), on food (as opposed to alcohol) intake, and even sleep deprivation – all likely to increase psychological tension and drama. We watch people who already often have poor impulse control put themselves on display so that their notoriety or fame (if there is still a difference) can be leveraged to earn them, and certainly others, money. Producers, in essence, are paying people to behave badly. On the other hand, some prominent RTV stars have learnt to leverage their exposure to their advantage. Those on a series like *The Real Housewives* command high salaries and in their renewal negotiations are extracting profit from viewer interest, this in addition to many business ventures based on their TV fame. Some use their TV celebrity to find others they can exploit: for example, "real housewife" Sonja Morgan has acquired multiple "interns" or unpaid staff. So who is exploiting whom one might ask?

Nevertheless, RTV participants work within many restrictions and must obey explicit and tacit conventions, including not complaining about, pointing to, or finding fault with the filming process or its results. Most fundamentally, they are asked to perform certain kinds of affective work and to produce the immaterial labor that relies upon an individual's personality, intellect, and emotion (Hearn 2010; Andrejevic 2011; Grindstaff 2011a). This activity can be seen more broadly in the service and symbolic economies, its increase blurring the line between economic, cultural, and political spheres. Drawing on Marxist political theorists Hardt and Negri, Alison Hearn (2010) notes how this demand for a commodifiable personality and affect results in a form of self-branding of the employee. As she also observes, RTV unmistakably models this commodification of personal life experience and the subject's attempts to benefit from it.

Integrated advertising

RTV attracts its fair share of regular spot ads in commercial breaks but what is distinctive, especially in American programming, is its experimentation in branded entertainment or the integration of advertising into program content to produce *advertainment* (Deery 2004a). As I've suggested elsewhere, one of reality TV's strongest claims to being real is when it represents the reality of an increasingly sponsored and branded life, an experience that this programming presents as often benign as well as inevitable (Deery 2012). Much RTV normalizes the idea that there is always a commercial motive behind things, that there is no free lunch, and that those who pay deserve a voice: hence, even charitable shows function as advertising vehicles. In this way viewers are being acclimatized to the inevitability of capitalist exchange and to the ubiquity of the market. But, more specifically, RTV reflects *the PR effect*, whereby hidden or oblique commercial forces increasingly determine what we see in life or on screen and it becomes difficult to find anything that is not generated by and for commercial purposes (Deery 2012). PR, I suggest, is the great *dark matter* of contemporary culture, exerting a considerable but invisible pull. So when the commercialization of programming is masked or unacknowledged, this authentically reflects a similar masking of our experience of reality elsewhere. To complain that reality TV is deceptive in this regard may therefore be an exercise in nostalgia.

The commercial element is not an add-on but integral and generative. It creates and it validates. Certainly part of the motive for developing RTV, as conceived by the likes of John de Mol, was to find programming that would suit advertising needs in a post-advertising, convergent environment. "*Survivor* is as much a marketing vehicle as it is a television show," says its producer Mark Burnett (Sager 2001) and Fox Entertainment Television president Gail Berman said of *American Idol*'s inception: "One of the tasks we set for ourselves was to find a reality show that was ad-friendly" (Battaglio 2002) – which they certainly did, given that the show's finale now reportedly charges more for advertising spots than the almighty Super Bowl (Caudle 2011: 186). However, as well as selling simple commercial breaks, RTV producers have long been interested in models where there is no break and where the advertising doesn't look like advertising.

Product placement

Product placement is integrated, indirect, and unannounced advertising designed to be particularly effective in a media environment where direct advertising can be evaded (DVRs, etc.).[4] Advertisers pay for their client's product to be placed within the show content where they hope it will both fit in and stand out. Generally the aim is for a seamless and "organic" placement where the product is recognized but not the fact that someone paid to make it appear.

However, most viewers do recognize and discuss placement: often with irritation but at other times accepting that this is part of how programming is funded. Some surveys suggest that there is more tolerance for plugs on RTV than in other programming (Hill 2005; Jenkins 2006: 88; Gillan 2011: 183). Placement is part of the staged nature of RTV, but again it can pass as realistic to the extent that brands are increasingly present in real life. Certainly RTV producers have been enthusiastic and on successful shows there tends to be more, not less, placement over time. With syndication being only a dim possibility, they are under pressure to maximize revenues from each episode's initial broadcast. Industry research also indicates that product placement produces a better recall rate than regular television commercials (Jacobson and Mazur 1995: 69); hence, its presence is now tracked by Nielsen and by companies such as iTVX that attempt to measure the effectiveness of brand integration.

Placement can be of physical objects, services, trademarks, or music. There is also a growing trend of what we might call *self-placement*, where participants deliberately insert themselves into a series in order to advertise themselves as a brand: so the broadest category of placement may be of people. However, placement is more commonly associated with the incorporation of branded objects, a practice that RTV has long promoted, though the degree to which is it adopted depends on regulation. In 2006, the European Union allowed product placement but with genre restrictions: placements could not appear in news, current affairs, or children's programming. At the time of writing, product placement is allowed with restrictions in Britain and other European countries and with blessing in the US. In the UK, many types of products (e.g., cigarettes or alcohol) may not be placed anywhere in domestically produced programming. On commercial channels, product placement must be editorially justified and not unduly prominent, and the broadcaster must display a double "P" symbol at the start and end of the program and after each commercial break.[5]

When placement is allowed, advertisers may be involved early on in the production process and be an important part of the initial funding or even program conception. Indeed, producer Mark Burnett makes a case that advertisers can be part of the creative process, asserting that they can have good ideas and work more collaboratively than network bosses (Littleton 2004). On the other hand, many kinds of product can be inserted not long before filming because of the relative lack of scripting or plot. RTV can easily and positively accommodate a placed product as a prize, a reward, a form of aid, or something recommended by an expert. These affective contexts obviously generate desire and focus attention. In many instances, the placed products are essential, for without them there would be no show. A more unusual scenario is what I have termed Spartan placement (Deery 2004a), where objects are placed in a barren or limited landscape and thus avoid the clutter of other advertisements or products. Within the confines of the *Big Brother* house or the faux primitivism of *Survivor*, with its almost surreal juxtaposition of natural scarcity and manufactured luxury items, players are keenly interested in the good's use value (e.g., to satisfy hunger) but also recognize its sign value: brands have become part of a culture's collective identity, so when eating Doritos the stranded players are also connecting to their home culture. Of course, one possible risk in endurance scenarios is that competitors will articulate ideas about people being ultimately more important than stuff, and this does sometimes happen. Still, no one rejects or criticizes the bag of Doritos and such remarks are undercut by the fact that the speakers are temporarily undergoing deprivation in order to win a boatload of money.

When there is more than a fleeting camera glance, the product's status can change from object to event, from incidental to key narrative component. An example of this *performative placement* (Deery 2014) is when competitors are asked to create a campaign to sell a product and by featuring this task they do, in fact, advertise the product on national TV (*The Apprentice*). Similarly, a show might feature the making of ads by fashion models. Or the competitive task may be to use a product, as when chefs are asked to feature a particular brand or appliance in their food preparation. There can be multiple layers of placement, some of it anticipatory. To take one example, *Fashion Star* (NBC 2012–13) is a clothing design competition where the winners' items are ready for purchase by the time the episode is aired (anticipated plug). In addition, store buyers gain publicity for their retail company by appearing as judges, and celebrity advisors promote their own fashion lines.

There can also be a form of *location placement*, as when *Top Chef* producers ask visitors bureaus and state offices for cash and other incentives to feature their location, though of course none of this is disclosed. Indeed, when it emerged that the Texas governor's office might have paid hundreds of thousands of dollars, the TV production company sued to prevent any official release of information. Another form of location-as-placement is the ritualistic timed excursion to a named store to gather ingredients for creative projects (*Project Runway*; *Top Chef*). The retailer becomes part of the action and its quality and range of goods is dutifully extolled. Placement therefore shapes and even distorts content: it will affect a show if nothing else because scenes containing plugs will more likely make the final cut. But placement can add realism too. In *The Apprentice*, in the midst of stage-set boardrooms and ego-boosting performances, some of the more real elements are the involvement of corporations whose representatives introduce real-life needs and parameters. Where placements can undermine the truth claims and even premise of the programming is when an expert recommends a product or service and the viewer has no way of knowing if this is only because they've been paid to do so.

Designer ads are commercial spots tailored to a particular series, often extending or mirroring its content by featuring program participants or themes. These are an expensive proposition usually reserved for the huge ratings of the Super Bowl, but they have also appeared around some popular RTV shows. For example, *American Idol* contestants have regularly appeared in mini-dramas functioning as spot ads for Ford, while Coke's agency created a "good luck to finalists" spot that aired moments before the winner announcement and 24 hours later produced a congratulatory ad for the winner. On the British *Pop Idol*,

Nestlé mirrored content by introducing singing chocolate bars in its designer ads and inviting viewers to vote for their favorite chocolate idol. Another mirroring of content can be seen when a character from a home design show, *Flipping Out* (Bravo 2007–) appeared in an ad for Glade "plug-in" air fresheners, and this spot ad (about home design) is followed by a regular ad for the same product (talk about plug-ins).

Sponsors and donors

One of the earliest methods for monetizing TV was sponsorship, a technique inherited from early radio. This offered advertisers prestige and some editorial control (McAllister 1996), but the practice diminished after the quiz show scandals of the 1950s when it was discovered that some sponsored shows were rigged to maximize ratings. In subsequent decades, sponsorship was rare and mostly of live sporting events by companies who were otherwise banned from direct TV advertising (tobacco). Recently there has been a modest revival in certain types of reality TV, not for reasons of legal regulation but because of changing technology and the need for branded content. As in the past, sponsors usually finance a show up front and overtly because they wish their brand to be recognized as a magnanimous partner. Many sign on for an entire series and others fund a program segment. Most packages include spot ads or designer ads and product placement. Some extend their sponsorship to the broadcaster's website.

Some RTV makeovers are significant because they elevate sponsorship to donorship, to the charitable handing over of goods and services to individuals in need. This foregrounded gesture, which amalgamates gift and market economies, can accomplish two things at once: produce appropriately targeted and organically embedded product placement (items people really need) and generate good publicity for the donor. Another corporation, the broadcaster, also gains some useful PR. The subjects who are being helped trade their privacy for goods and services. Donors trade goods and services for the opposite, for publicity. Either way, the *currency is media exposure*.[6] More broadly, these actions bolster the image of a prosocial caring capitalism whose privatized solutions are part of a PR-motivated expansion into social entrepreneurship: seen on formats from *Extreme Makeover: Home Edition* to *Undercover Boss* (see Ouellette and Hay 2008; Hollows and Jones 2010; Biressi 2011; Deery 2012). This stance is not new, but currently the pressure is mounting for capitalist organizations to display Corporate Social Responsibility (with an official abbreviation of CSR) and some RTV formats provide popular and cost-effective sites for this kind of promotion.[7] Corporate donorship is an effective and affective branding technique because it manifests as an intimate transaction whose valuable connectivity makes viewers give their (paid for) attention where it is due, almost as a matter of politeness. No dollar amounts are mentioned, but donating to a TV show represents not so much a transcendence of commerce as an oblique recirculation that highlights a neo-feudalism behind contemporary privatization. Reality TV makes the most of the fact that private aid, unlike public assistance, is voluntary, personal, subjectively selected, and under no obligation to be comprehensive. In their promotion of privatization, conservative leaders from Bush to Cameron have emphasized charitable volunteerism in place of public support and on RTV programs there is no longer even the expectation of government help. Viewers are encouraged to applaud generous benefactors and needy but grateful recipients, while the system that produced these asymmetries remains unexamined. The fact that large corporations are helping only a handful of people is not criticized; rather the small scale becomes heartwarming. Richard Sennett (1992 [1974]) lamented this kind of sentimental depoliticization when the tyranny of intimacy replaces public action with private feeling (p. 339). On makeover TV, the paucity of support is capitalized on, via mediation, because it generates drama. The thrill is greater when one individual helps another than if we were observing bureaucrats dispensing standard aid to thousands. Privatization and drama become mutually supportive (Deery 2012).

Web integration

Show-associated websites may also function as significant commercial locations, though their potential is still being explored. To begin, online space can be sold to any interested advertiser and each viewer visit constitutes an advertisement for the show. Viewers, too, can build their own associated sites and commoditize them by attracting advertising or by selling the URL. Broadcaster websites can be used to advertise upcoming shows with short video teasers. Or they may offer exclusive extra footage, an access that can be tied to retail sales: for instance, Energizer batteries gave the purchaser a code they could use to access online audition tapes (Roscoe 2004: 188). There have also been experiments in tying second-screen apps to TV watching; for example, an app for mobile devices like Zeebox (launched in the UK in 2011) provides information synchronized to the TV show such as photos, tweets, polls, web links, news, bios. Again, this method can also sell aggregated audience data back to broadcasters and studios.

In 2004, NBC and Bravo engaged a specialist company to "shop-enable" a range of shows by offering fans "a fully branded, customized, interactive experience"[8] – that is, they facilitate the sale of items related to the show. Much of this commercial activity is still relatively loosely organized and its prominence varies from one show site to another. But we can see that the selling of show-branded goods further extends and commodifies the experience of watching TV, providing a material link to screen images; occasionally producers sell off original show items in charity auctions so the fetishistic link is even stronger (*The Real World*; *Survivor*).[9] Purchasing merchandise becomes for some a totemistic activity, expressing group identity, loyalty, engagement, a sense of belonging. On RTV the practice took off with the first wave of gamedocs like *Survivor* and continues today, with some series attracting particularly extensive and intense levels of merchandising, most of which is transacted online but some of which appears in retail stores (currently *Duck Dynasty* merchandising is so extensive as to rival major players like Disney). Typically broadcaster sites sell everything from mugs to mouse pads and the youthful audience of many RTV series are likely comfortable with online shopping. Some selling of merchandise is presented as a form of interactivity, as a dialogue between show and viewers: for example, fans send in photos of themselves using products with captions that suggest merchandise is being produced in response to their requests. Another motivator is loyalty: as with sports fans, *Survivor* viewers are exhorted to show their loyalty to their tribe/team by donning branded clothing.

Commodifying personal relationships

If RTV demonstrates anything it is that *all mediation has the potential to commodify experience.* But specific to RTV is the selling of what is intimate and ordinarily not publicly accessible. The thrill of transgression is intensified because access is being granted to real people's private lives, this being more of a novelty than access to fictional lives. RTV therefore raises some central concerns of contemporary society such as: what, today, is considered private, how valuable is privacy, and who should manage it? Privacy is a shifting concept undergoing considerable stress, some of which is being applied by RTV. Ultimately, this programming is testing how far the marketplace can expand into the private realm and convert new areas into the public and privatized. As twin legal concepts, private and public have changed meaning historically and from society to society. Today, "private" is often associated with the idea of property, which makes trading privacy as a commodity perhaps not so strange. This association is played out on RTV if, for example, we observe the parallels between home and body makeovers: the temporary transfer of ownership rights, the similar architectural rhetoric, and the notion of the body as an external (and alienable) commercial site (Deery 2006, 2012). As with home makeovers, subjects lease out their body to others who benefit financially from the transaction – a particularly stark illustration of how under capitalism the body becomes something one can invest in both economically and psychologically to produce an instrumental relation to the self. Similarly, private home properties are seen as reflecting one's identity (*Four Houses*, TLC 2012) and so the series *Interior Therapy* (Bravo 2012–) proposes changing one's house design as a way to change human relationships. Many RTV programs, in fact, promote *consumption* as a form of *mediation* through which social relations are reproduced.

Sometimes participants reshuffle the usual hierarchy of privacy and access: when they reveal on camera deep secrets they've kept from friends and family, or when they appear without makeup or after surgery, images they don't necessarily share with those close to them. Later their actions will be before millions, yet they ask others present to leave the room so they may exchange secrets or "have more privacy." This accustoming people to occupy a *close distance* to other people may be one of RTV's more profound and lasting effects.

Reality programming empowers commercial agents to survey and discipline subjects in ways that would be seen as highly objectionable, as well as illegal, if performed by noncommercial, governmental forces. But, as we know, commercialization isn't just something that is done *to* participants; they frequently have their own commercial agenda and are quite happy to market themselves as a brand (Hearn 2008; also Ouellette and Hay 2008; Redden 2009; B. Weber 2009; Palmer 2011). This used to be a hidden or only half-acknowledged motive, but increasingly participants talk about their TV appearance as a deliberate strategy and a form of "work." They know that even bad publicity can be leveraged to promote other business concerns, so if they didn't have something to publicize going in, most *do* by the time they have accumulated some TV capital. All of which works against any "fly-on-the-wall" authenticity and suggests that commercialization can undermine the media product. Many of the women on luxury docusoaps afford their lifestyle in part by selling its props (clothing, alcohol, jewelry), so the TV show *creates the reality it sells* by allowing participants to capitalize on their being mediated. While filming, they mimic corporate participation by creating their own product placements and by staging pseudo-events to promote their own businesses: indeed, Bethenny Frankel leveraged a huge business deal by making her brand creation the theme of her show. Increasing numbers extend this promotion into blogs and tweets where reality stars can earn additional money for mentioning other brands. Several also pitch their own brands on another form of interactive TV, the shopping channel, or show up off screen for paid "personal appearances" (a pure example of being paid to be themselves).

Another commercial avenue for participants is selling magazines and tabloids information about their ongoing lives and maybe even more intimate realities than those displayed on TV. Indeed, there is an increasingly important symbiosis between celebrity magazines and RTV production, some of which is managed by professional PR agencies. In *After Shock: Heidi and Spencer* (E! 2013), the infamous ex-*Hills* stars admitted to fabricating tabloid stories about bankruptcy and divorce solely to generate income. Some participants go to the press before discussing personal matters with family and friends, who are then hurt because displaced due to financial considerations. The impetus to turn TV appearance to profit can generate drama within the show also, when one person's attempt to hawk their business interests causes jealousy among other cast members. So although not presented as a game, it turns out that a docusoap *is*, and the competition for commercial promotion and contract renewal powerfully structure the drama both within and beyond the show.

Being on TV makes prior relationships more transactional or, alternatively, makes instrumental relationships into forms of friendship. Friends become commercial opportunities, and commercial providers are treated as ersatz friends. Some formats aim to make TV arrangements into serious relationships but usually without success once filming ends (matchmaking and dating programs). If any of this process is considered unsavory and gets viewers excited, then so be it. Again, RTV doesn't have to be approved of to be successful. Take the Kardashians. They have become a lightning rod for disgust at a market-based understanding of human relationships. They are seen as people who are living their lives just to make profitable TV; they are therefore not filming a *life* being *lived* so much as *living* a *mediated life*. Many viewers perceive a whorish element to this self-promotion (they refer to the mother as the "pimp momager"). Some talk about commercial retaliation such as boycotting advertisers or Kardashian business interests and indeed thousands have signed such online petitions. There are concerns that this family can no longer distinguish business from personal matters and that a mother is exploiting her offspring (including sexually) for commercial gain. (Khloe Kardashian once joked that a child born into her family is like a slave who is obliged to contribute to the family business.[10]) There is a similar condemnation of both producers and parents in *Toddlers and Tiaras* or *Jon & Kate Plus 8*, where offspring appear to be treated as business opportunities. Indeed, RTV minors are legally less protected than child actors on more regulated and unionized programming. More generally, much RTV programming tests just how far people will go for material gain. For example, is it OK to prioritize money over love, to surrender planning important life events in return for financial aid, to deceive and betray in order to win a prize? A sizeable portion of reality programming provokes both viewers and participants to squirm about prioritizing profit over other values – which suggests that commercialization has not been fully embraced in all areas of life.

Consumer society

Consumption is more than buying stuff. It is not solely an economic activity but also involves aspirations, desires, creativity, and so on. Consumerism – the belief that people should spend lots of money on goods and services – is an ideology that affects, among other things, power, law, identity, and ethics.[11] Reality TV not only benefits from but also often promotes consumerism. In common parlance, and certainly in learned discourse, the act of shopping tends to be denigrated or thought of as trivial, whereas much RTV programming attempts to raise its status by suggesting that shopping is an art, a strategy, an expression of love, a valuable expertise in a postfeminist, neoliberal world. One clear indicator of the influence of consumerism on everyday experience is the notion of defining one's identity in terms of a lifestyle, an advertising concept from the 1980s that markets an assemblage of goods and services. The persistent makeover impulse in much RTV ratifies this concept and attests to the transformative and therapeutic power of correct and coherent consumer choices in styling a life. Individuals on RTV are being made over as consumers and in their attitude to consumption. Beyond promoting specific products, this programming establishes an entire ethos of consumption as life-affirming, creative, and essential, whatever the budget or time constraints. An *imperative TV* insists on the transformation of real life, in accordance with the central message of advertising, which is that we should (1) improve our situation and (2) do so through consumption. The result is a consumer-based *mass individualism* that makes daily performances self-conscious and self-monitored, as in the heightened version of reality TV. The advertising imperative to always make a good impression therefore links performance to commercialization and to neoliberalism. In response to this media stimulus to improve and scrutinize the self, sociologist Nikolas Rose (1996) notes the rise of an expert class who, whether clinical psychologists or style "gurus," appears to be wholly in our service and in fulfillment of our own desires. But their dispersal of institutional power is, of course, a fundamental form of socialization, for, as Baudrillard observed, consumption is a collective behavior and a system of values, so today's citizens require a "social training in consumption" comparable to nineteenth-century training in matters of production (1998 [1970]: 81). It seems RTV is contributing to this training – or even to our perception that we need this training. While viewers critique specific advice or plugs, Katherine Sender (2012) found that they accept the general consumer ethos, the faith that consuming can fix things and improve one's life.

Attitudes to consumption are telling because they are a materialization of more abstract values and ideologies. In the US, RTV often supports the aspirational mythology of the American Dream. Makeovers, competitions, advice programming, all suggest that upward mobility is something to aim for, is within reach, and is most obviously demonstrated in material acquisition. But this is really the cruel optimism that Lauren Berlant (2011) underlines, where people are encouraged to cling to post-war ideologies of the good life and of meritocracy that are no longer supported by a neoliberal capitalism. The original American Dream, as envisioned by James Truslow Adams in *The Epic of America* (1931), referred to an equality of opportunity that would allow a large middle class to flourish, whereas many of RTV's rescue makeovers actually signal the steady evisceration of this class. Adams' dream was not simply of acquiring material possessions but, more importantly, social justice (Deery 2012: 106–7). Yet reality shows generally reinforce the consumerist interpretation that has since taken hold.

Several American series feature fantasies of affluence and the joy and liberation of shopping without a budget, whether by delighted makeover recipients or privileged offspring. Wealthy families are open about expressing their love by buying each other things: for example, a repeated and sentimental ritual on luxury docusoaps is someone buying their teenager an expensive car or extravagant birthday party. Or, repeatedly, we witness a bride "falling in love" with a wedding dress once she finds "the one" and then, in an affective override of financial concerns, she ignores her budget.[12] Romance is thus thoroughly commodified as well as commodities being imbued with romance. But not just romance. Shopping expresses all kinds of love and is a time for social bonding with friends, family – and of course TV experts. Again we see *consumption as a form of mediation*, mediating our role in society. Goods help create social networks and are given value by the emotions that circulate through them.

A more masculine approach to consumption is in programming that emphasizes the excitement and adventure of commercial exchange, its centrality to human culture, even its educational and historical significance. Whereas the more genteel *Antiques Roadshow* has long guarded its distance from trade as a matter of prestige, the latest batch of RTV programming focuses on price and profit. What we might call trade shows film dramatic interpersonal negotiations for items that appeal to the hobbyist in a developed economy (*American Pickers*; *Pawn Stars*). For example, "pickers" fill a particular niche by searching for old or abandoned objects in private ownership that can be sold in a retail store. They re-purpose objects by making the previously functional into the artifactual; for example, old advertising signs that were used to fetishize other objects now become fetishized themselves. In these contexts, shopping is validated and its objects revered because they are antiques (or "mantiques") and part of "collections" (for many, a good rationale to keep buying). The traders pause to produce facts and educational nuggets. They extol the triumphs of American manufacturing. They curate and save the past. *American Pickers*, like *Pawn Stars*, appears on the History Channel, a broadcaster that is increasingly artifactual, telling history through commodities and turning history into a commodity: hence its slogan "History. Made every day." As a demonstration of how RTV affects real-life commerce, *American Pickers* has apparently boosted sales of affordable Americana and tilted the antique market toward "mantiques" for "man caves." The shop featured in *Pawn Stars* has seen a huge increase in customers and is now a tourist attraction selling its own branded merchandise. However, the popularity of *Storage Wars* has increased attendance at auctions and pushed up prices to the detriment of TV participants already in the business.

High consumption

Other reality programming depicts hyper-consumption and its theatrical or fantastic dimensions. Bravo TV, in particular, specializes in high-end, glossy shows that attract what it calls "affluencers" (affluent influencers), savvy viewers attractive to advertisers who enjoy shows that reinforce the thrill, the romance, the gratification of luxury spending. Here and elsewhere, RTV series whet our appetites for haute cuisine (*Top Chef*) or haute couture (*Project Runway*) and reinforce the current mainstreaming of luxury brands, what I've termed the Godiva effect after the mass distribution of a formerly exclusive chocolatier's brand (Deery 2012). Common across several broadcasters is the wedding, after house buying for most people the biggest consumer ritual of their lives. The fruition of years of consumer training, the wedding emboldens even ordinary people to engage in positional consumption to establish temporary high status (castles and limos). These grand potlatch displays (Mauss 1990 [1950]) demonstrate the deep symbolic meaning accorded to consumer choices and the creativity and power of sanctioned excess. Weddings are a great fit for reality TV given that they come with their own liturgy/script and virtually guarantee drama, not least because of the license to spend. They typically hit the sweet spot of reality TV, where events are both actual and fantastic, authentic and dramatic.

This does not mean that all RTV shows simply promote maximum consumption: some are ambivalent and others suggest that high levels of consumption can be dysfunctional. Occasionally there is some price-tagging where viewers are shown the price of objects as a kind of mute editorial comment, but this is rare outside trade shows (real estate or pawn stores). The more negative portraits are implicit. Many viewers recognize that the big spenders are prone to narcissism, selfishness, greed, and so on. They tend to have an exaggerated self-importance and when, as many do, they get into debt, viewers take the opportunity to roundly criticize them for over-reaching. But if participants can afford their expenditures then many viewers report being happy to vicariously enjoy their wealthy lifestyle. Some practices, however, are framed as entirely unhealthy and even as requiring full psychiatric intervention. Series with titles like *Spendaholics* (BBC3 2005–7) and *My Shopping Addiction* (Oxygen 2012–) obviously label hyperconsumption an addictive behavior. The latter employs psychologists who usually determine that subjects suffer from low self-esteem or lack of fulfillment. But even more spectacular anxieties about over-consumption have emerged in shows about typically lower-middle-class "hoarders," whose inability to control their expenditure is depicted as pathological and dangerous (*Hoarders*; *Hoarding: Buried Alive*). Hoarders are usually seen as overwhelmed by their possessions. Their compulsive behavior and failure as rational consumers endanger their physical well-being (fire hazards, injuries) and personal relationships (divorce, child custody). These programs impress upon us that shopping ought not to be trivialized but rather respected for its impact and consequences. Meanwhile, the TV shows cash in on the spectacle of excess, requiring exposure before offering aid.

Low consumption

Consumer dysfunction can also take the form of under-consumption, another aberrant behavior that RTV can capitalize on. Low levels of consumption can be voluntary or involuntarily, self-initiated or imposed. We see in shows like *Extreme Cheapskates* (TLC 2012–) a form of consumer anorexia. Subjects appear to feel they are triumphing over regular market forces but obviously the judgmental title and approach positions them differently. The focus is on the sordid details of people's bathroom or food habits and how their compulsion adversely affects others. These are not people who are too poor to consume – this could introduce uncomfortable pathos and even politics – but those who are not consuming properly.

Other examples of frugality have reflected a recessionary cycle in the larger economy, whether the self-explanatory *Extreme Couponing* (2010–), shows about foreclosed home sales (*Property Wars*, Discovery 2012–), buying marked down retail items (*I Found the Gown*, TLC 2012–), family budget cutbacks (*Downsized*, WE tv 2010–11) or religiously inspired frugal living (*19 Kids and Counting*). Some men try to generate income frontier-style in shows like *Gold Rush* or *Ax Men*, where Diane Negra notes the gendered contrasts between "a feminized thrift and a masculinized risk taking" (2013: 123). Other shows teach everyone how to economize: from *Economy Gastronomy* (BBC2 2009) to Jamie Oliver's *Money Saving Meals* (C4 2013). Already established high-end consumption series reflected the larger economy post 2008. There was some tightening of belts and loss of business evident in docusoaps and real estate shows: hence *Property Ladders* (C4 2001–) became *Property Snakes and Ladders* in 2009. In particular, the British seem partial to economic discipline and advice shows in a no-nonsense maternal form like *The Fairy Jobmother*

(C4 2010–; Lifetime 2010) or *Benefit Busters* (C4 2009) and some series offer training and rehab to increase consumer literacy: *Superscrimpers* (C4 2011), *Bank of Mum and Dad* (BBC2 2004; SoapNet 2009) and *You're Cut off* (VH1 2010), the latter two offering a sort of detox for young spendthrifts. Also resonant with a fragile economy and job insecurity is the constant elimination mechanism in so many reality formats. During the recession, shows featuring the business world were explicitly placed in the context of an economic contraction; opening voiceovers spoke of people needing a second chance after losing their jobs (the US *Apprentice*) or losing faith in corporate America (*Undercover Boss*, C4 2009–; CBS 2010–).

More voluntary low consumption can be due to environmental concerns: this is particularly evident in Britain in, for example, *It's Not Easy Being Green* (BBC2 2006, 2007), *The Real Good Life* (ITV 2005) and *How to Live a Simple Life* (BBC2 2010) (see, e.g., Thomas 2008) and in Australia *Eco-House Challenge* and *Carbon Cops* (Lewis 2011: 86). What Heather Nunn calls "retreat TV" features those who downshift because they are ideologically disillusioned with high consumption (Nunn 2011: 175). She notes that these shows decouple improvement and consumption but still focus on individualized solutions rather than the broader social context (p. 176). Other formats portray groups adhering to low consumption on principle; for example, disciplined sects like the Amish are exotic for their deliberate lack of exposure to consumer society. But, more generally, whether high or low, consumption is key to one's identity and status: this is the broad message of much RTV programming.

Business opportunity

Finally, another trend in recent programming is the business opportunity and the business makeover. Most shows offer positive images of the desire to make a profit and offer advice to those who are not currently maximizing their assets. Experts counsel the middle classes on how to pull themselves up and achieve the

Dream (*Ramsay's Kitchen Nightmares*, C4 2004–9, Fox 2007–; *Tabatha Takes Over*, Bravo 2008–). Family-owned businesses typically suffer from mismanagement but the owner's heart is usually seen as in the right place. After issuing some necessary criticism, the expert generally asserts the authority of the owners and dispensability of employees. When, alternatively, drama stems from the brutality of more impersonal competition (*Apprentice*; *Dragon's Den*; *Shark Tank*), viewers are invited to admire the opportunities afforded by a less sentimental but still meritocratic capitalism.

Conclusion

Reality TV's prevalence is undeniably due to economics: people *do* watch it, but there wouldn't be so much of it if it cost more to make. As a low-risk and easily commercialized product it has been readily embraced by the media industry. Among other things, it enabled more niche broadcasting, flexible scheduling, and profitable interactivity when these became a matter of survival. In many instances, RTV producers have been at the forefront of experiments in integrative advertising. Moreover, reality TV not only commodifies and privatizes the experiences it represents, but also frequently gives its viewers cues for how to negotiate a consumer culture. It validates consumer life styling and makes the act of consumption vital and spectacular, whether wholesome (usually) or hazardous (less often).

5

Gender and Race

Much of the attraction of RTV likely comes down to curiosity about other people in an increasingly anonymous and atomistic society. Its viewing access commercializes the age-old desire to know what the neighbors are up to, or to assess how normal or strange we or others are. RTV offers vicarious relationships and parasocial engagement; indeed, most formats are character-driven and possess little in the way of impressive dialogue or intricate plot. Some programs can trace their appeal back to early freak shows or recreational visits to the asylum, others to the ancient and vicarious thrill of watching individuals compete. Many series aim to appeal to young adults – not coincidentally, those whom advertisers seek – by attempting to break taboos or by offering advice on forming one's identity or improving one's love or career prospects (one survey found that younger viewers like RTV 4:1 over those aged 55 and older; see Bennett et al. 2009: 142). Personal identity is a general orientation because as a "first person media" (Dovey 2000) RTV hones in on the intimate and the subjective. But there is a *sacrificial* tinge to some of it. Participants who have signed away fundamental rights play the role of scapegoats. They are ordinary but singled out.

At the same time, there are other ethical distortions at play. One effect is perhaps excessive honesty, when producers reward people for being frank to the point of rudeness or even cruelty. After delivering hurtful remarks, speakers frequently defend their upsetting others by saying: "Well, I was just being honest" or "at least

I said it to your face," not recognizing the need for moderating behavior according to circumstances (i.e., decorum). Participants appear to believe that characterizing lack of restraint as honesty allows them to say or do whatever they want: and given the drama they generate it is unlikely anyone on the production staff will argue otherwise.

When it comes to social identity, scholars generally maintain that media representations are crucial in providing frameworks and creating reference groups. The next chapter will consider class as a social marker but this chapter focuses on gender and race – which, for clarity's sake, are considered separately – with a view to highlighting broad topics that are particularly pertinent to reality television: among them performance, dramatic irony, non-fictional stereotyping, body imagery, and consumption.[1] In addition, this chapter offers models for categorizing types of media incorporation, identifies gender-inflected programming, and underlines the commercial and dramaturgical motives that shape representation. The potentially subversive nature of RTV performances also becomes apparent. For a striking thing about reality TV is the *self-consciousness* of ethnic, racial, and gender identities and their being performed by *real people* – albeit to fit the needs of a TV show. It is easy to see how this reflexivity could underline the performativity of these roles beyond television: that is, how we all play gender or race and how identities are formed by being performed. Reality TV is an extrovert form that attracts extrovert characters. It encourages not just performance but what Kavka (2014a) calls the exhibitionist "flaunting" of gender or other identities. Amplification and self-consciousness are key. Moreover, several formats foreground the significance of improving or promoting this self-conscious self and so resonate with ideas in high and low discourse about individual enterprise and the self-as-project. In many instances RTV enacts esoteric postmodern (Butler) or late modern (Giddens) thinking in sociology and cultural studies about unstable and malleable selves.[2]

Some formats focus on collective identities, often representing overtly labeled subcultural groups such as the Amish or gypsies or cops. But most focus on individual identity and often changes in, or to, this identity, whether through a trajectory of career advancement, outside intervention, social experiment, or physical makeover. Some narratives raise the specter of there being no core identity and so the need to create one, others claim to find or enhance an inner self. In any case, identity is often self-consciously on display; it is stretched, examined, created, altered, broken down, or mocked. Many programs feature enterprising, ambitious, and "big" personalities, some of whom have specific talents (they sing, dance, cook) and others who simply have the talent, if that's what it is, of being extrovert, outrageous, and uninhibited: in other words, they have the talent for creating drama without need of writers. Another characteristic of much RTV is that the difference between self-identity and social perception is mined for dramatic irony: viewers enjoy the drama that comes from the gap between how subjects apparently view themselves and how others judge them.

Reality producers are not shy about creating or perpetuating hyperbolic portraits: the hollow trophy wife, the sexy guido, the Black diva, the flamboyant gay. These become strong flavors that attract different audiences – whether through close identification or distant curiosity – so it is a *commercial diversity born of the niche broadcasting of differentiated products*. It is also a diversity based on stereotypes and, while as a cognitive shortcut stereotyping is a common communication technique, inaccuracies become particularly harmful when difference is given a moral significance. This is something RTV exploits. Its mode raises particularly acute questions about moral charge and accountability given that the stereotype is not a fictional creation but the portrait of a real person. Will this validate the stereotype more conclusively? Or, in a circular fashion, will a real person be judged more realistic if they fit a previous stereotype promulgated by the media? Certainly, RTV viewers quite often discuss if people are being stereotyped, why this might be, and what social effects it might have. As RTV solidifies its favorite templates, people audition and are cast to continue to play these now well-known roles whether or not the participants themselves catch on to this assignment. And since RTV shows don't have writers who could be held accountable for lines delivered and who might feel obliged to be "politically correct," reality participants air remarks that would not be acceptable elsewhere on the schedule, remarks that provoke heated viewer engagement. The nature of RTV production therefore allows stereotypes and prejudices to be flushed out and criticized, or condoned, or both.

Engendering serious social debate is, however, probably not first in the reality producer's mind. Rather they are tapping into something as old as the commercial possibilities of circuses and sideshows. Today's entertainments cash in on the theatricalization of mental instability and the spectacle of outrageous behavior. People insult each other, backstab, cheat, lie. Being aggressive or mean or vindictive attracts attention and RTV participants either know this going in, or think they will come across much better than they do. Either way, when they emerge as villains they tend to be rewarded with contract renewals and expanding brand exposure. This process of leveraging bad behavior appears to be getting more self-conscious and widespread. Subjects increasingly embrace labels like "bitch," "diva," or "bridezilla," terms that were previously matters of shame. Their TV status suggests that there is power in getting attention, any way you can. But of course the economic rewards for the TV display don't usually carry over into real life and this can affect real-life relationships.

One of RTV's most central effects may be its mainstreaming of what was previously considered abnormal or taboo. In recent decades, many societies have congratulated themselves on changing attitudes to physical difference or disability – at least in legislative initiatives. But it looks like the desire to stare at the abnormal continues and is fed by RTV. The debate is whether this is ever done with sympathy and respect. It could be argued that people with dwarfism, for example, are quite sensitively portrayed on current reality shows and are admired for successfully carving out their own accommodation, both socially and architecturally, in custom-built environments (*Little People, Big World*; *The Little Couple*). People with physical or mental disabilities add a twist to regular formats, as in *The Undateables* (C4 2012–) or *Britain's Missing Top Model* (BBC3 2008), a modeling show for disabled women. Some of these programs may be evading social problems by ignoring or sugar-coating difficulties and prejudices for purposes of entertainment. The larger issue is how to adjudicate where helpful advocacy ends and a baser exploitation begins.

Self-as-project

Identity formation, or reformation, is a common theme across RTV, whether the focus is making over one's appearance, finding love, or becoming a star. Cultural theorists have noticed an increased interest in interiority in late modernity. More pragmatically, the advertisers that drive media production have long known that concerns such as these are good for business. Therefore, for both dramatic and economic reasons, there is a tendency on much RTV programming to regard the self as a project and one's identity as malleable (Giddens 1991; Rose 1996) – a fairly modern notion that is likely encouraged by media advertising constantly asking us to assess how we signify socially and how we might refashion this sign. Then there is the more recent preoccupation with building one's online persona through social media and ego-casting to the world. Reality TV's transformational formats stress that the self is something we must work upon, invest in, and optimize. The good citizen is the enterprising self who, through judicious consumer choices and promotion, strives to project the best image and performance of self (Rose 1996).[3] Ultimately, as we've seen, this process involves a form of self-branding (e.g., Hearn 2008; Ouellette and Hay 2008; B. Weber 2009).

There has been some discussion among viewers and scholars about whether RTV makeovers are creating a new identity or are revealing something largely fixed. Among TV participants there appears to be some agreement that inner and outer selves should match or cohere, but not about whether the inner drives the outer change or vice versa. Though there is insufficient space to go into detail here, we can say that some RTV makeovers appear to support the postmodern idea that we perform and create our identities, while others represent the process as finding and displaying a true inner and fixed self. Based on an audience study, Katherine Sender (2012) suggests that viewers want to see the latter and appear to endorse the romantic notion of finding the true inner self and authentic self-expression (p. 137). Although, as Brenda Weber (2009) points out, there is a tension and sometimes contradiction in TV makeovers when telling makeover subjects they should love who they are and indicating that they need to change. Another thing to consider is an overriding dramatic imperative: because of the requirements of *form* (short drama) and the *medium* (visual), there is on RTV little interest in gradual, non-visual, and more profound inner change. Producers are simply after a rapid alteration that is relatively cost-effective and therefore works for the medium and its investors.

Identity and consumption

There is some consensus among scholars that many RTV series are predicated on a reflexive, post-traditional society as described by sociologists such as Giddens, Beck, Bauman and others. In particular, makeover formats are indicative of the rise of the expert class and the cultural intermediary observed by Bourdieu, Rose, and Featherstone. As part of "the myth of the mediated center" (Couldry 2003), RTV plays its role in adjudicating and thereby defining a shared social reality. Much programming reinforces how personal life has taken on the values of the marketplace and the marketplace has become focused on personal life by underlining how in a post-scarcity society we establish our identity not so much through the goods we create as through those we consume (e.g., Baudrillard 1998 [1970]). Consumer choice is professed to be key to self-identity, to social well-being, to professional and romantic empowerment. But advice programming also suggests that the marketplace is now so complex that we need interpreters who know its codes. RTV showcases a new class of experts without clear credentials who mediate between goods and consumers. More pragmatically, it needs to establish such expertise in order to create drama-generating hierarchies. Style authorities appear confident that subjects can amass instant cultural capital without reference to any sociopolitical underpinnings: gender or age dictates some choices, but much else seems up for grabs. This expert intervention again illustrates the *commercialization of social relations*, where services that previously would have been performed by oneself or by friends and family are now professionalized and paid for. More often than not their claims to expertise are unquestioned by their TV subjects but, as audience studies reveal, viewers are quite capable of disputing or critiquing expert advice or authority (e.g., B. Weber 2009; Sender 2012; Skeggs and Wood 2012). Moreover, Annette Hill (2007) found that, even when they agree with it, viewers rarely adopt the advice proffered by TV experts.

Gender

When it comes to gender and race, we can begin by noting that RTV airs ideas and attitudes that more highly regarded programming mutes or avoids. The different perspectives among and between participants, and among and between viewers, mean that there is some variation in portrayals and impressions – although there are predominant trends. Questions we can ask about gender on RTV (not all of which are addressed here) include: How diverse are the representations? Is gender identity foregrounded or muted? How negative or positive are the portraits, and in whose terms? What kinds of stereotypes appear and have these modified over time? What is considered normative or aberrant? How do viewers of one gender regard a particular program? We can also identify different types of presence: single-gender; gender as novelty or twist (e.g., women on masculine shows); normal mix (e.g., gamedocs); and vital but ancillary (e.g., husbands on docusoaps). Occasionally, the theme of gender can be foregrounded: as when gamedoc teams are divided along gender lines, when *Wife Swap* deliberately examines contrasting gender roles, or when one gender is removed or given unusual control (*When Women Rule the World*, C4 2008). More generally, producers simply exaggerate gender distinctions if and when this generates eye-catching contrasts and conflicts – a commercial motive that can defamiliarize and denaturalize gender performance in general.

Feminine and masculine programming

In the niche markets of the cable era, gendered programming is one way to attract differentiated target audiences; indeed, some entire channels are branded as appealing to one gender.[4] More generally, RTV could be seen as a predominantly feminine output – as a feminization of factual forms like news or documentary that traditionally attract male viewers – because of a focus on domestic matters and unwaged labor, or on emotion and confessional revelation (Moseley 2000; Bignell 2005; Holmes and Jermyn 2014). Studies suggest that the majority of RTV viewers are women[5] and thus far many RTV series have focused on historically feminine concerns: appearance, interpersonal relations, social standing, consumption, parenting, cooking, romance, and milestone personal events like births and weddings. Many shows, especially the makeover/therapeutic and docusoap varieties, feature mostly female subjects. However, there has been a recent surge in masculine programming often with all-male casts directed at male viewers. Some of these appear to tap into a nostalgia for working-class manual labor, perhaps in part a response to metrosexual men seen elsewhere on RTV (Meltzer 2010). The attraction of shows about miners or fishermen may stem from the often reported crisis in masculinity in the wake of both feminism and the contraction of manufacturing jobs and skilled labor (Palmer 2014). Yet since RTV relies so much on affective labor, the whole phenomenon could be seen as mirroring the economic sectors in which women are disproportionately employed (Hochschild 1983; Andrejevic 2014; Grindstaff 2014). While they are in many ways exploitative, one could argue that RTV programs do at least recompense these forms of production and turn the domestic into an economic site: on the one hand, looking ahead to a blurring of work/leisure and, on the other, reconnecting the industrial age separation of spheres.[6]

Domestic politics

On RTV, patriarchal arrangements are still visible but some series refract or even question this status quo. For example, parenting shows go to the heart of everyday gender relations by addressing the division of domestic labor. Series such as *Wife Swap/ Trading Spouses* and *Supernanny* often suggest men take on more household and childcare responsibilities, although they also often scold mothers if they are thought to be too focused on a career and the program's premise clearly identifies home management with wives more than husbands. Indeed, motherhood is often flawed and problematic on reality TV. While there are some idealized portraits, most shows delve into women's many inadequacies. On nanny shows or series such as *Toddlers and Tiaras* or *Honey We're Killing the Kids*, examples of bad mothers inspire almost unanimous and vehement viewer condemnation. Wife swap shows, beyond the title's sexual innuendo, reference the tradition of regarding wives/future mothers as traded property[7] and indeed this series typically contrasts and assesses a wife's worth as a mother. A submissive and a dominant wife often swap positions – sometimes this results in vows to moderate both extremes, sometimes not.

Commentators have noted that dating and mating formats are often emphatically patriarchal and replay gender narratives of times past. They are also fundamentally transactional: several series suggest that people or love can be shopped for, tried on, and then rejected. From the women who agreed to marry a stranger just because he was wealthy on *Who Wants to Marry a Multi-Millionaire?* (Fox 2000) to any number of recent matchmaker or dating shows, a thin veneer of romance covers a fairly crude exchange: the trade between wealth and looks on *The Bachelor* is just a little more subtle than the shopping for mates on *The Millionaire Matchmaker*. In several "wife" docusoaps (*Footballers' Wives*; *Basketball Wives*) women of low rank marry wealthy men. As accessories or trophies, they display their husband's status through consumption but rarely do they execute this role with dignity or grace.

Jonathan Gray suggests that gender performances on dating shows are generally so over the top that they can be enjoyed as carnivalesque figures with no bearing on real-life decorum. They can be seen as ridiculing and undermining traditional performances of gender (2009: 275) – a caricature made explicit in the satiric spoof *Burning Love* (E! 2013). Crossdressers whose exaggerated mimicry points to gender performance appear on *America's Next Top Model* ("Miss J") or on *The Real Housewives of Atlanta* whose flamboyant hairstylists earned the spin-off show *Fashion Queens* (Bravo 2013–). An even stricter patriarchy is used to titillate modern viewers in a series like *My Big Fat Gypsy Wedding* where, in enclaves of almost pre-modern gender rules, girls are systematically undereducated, married off young (and virginal), and then devote their lives to domestic labor and submission. We see similar inequalities in religiously enforced patriarchies from fundamentalists to Mormons, though these series often downplay interpersonal male authority.

Many docusoap women are decorative and "kept," or appear to be. But as they acquire celebrity capital and grow more financially independent, they also exert more power in their marital arrangements. This leads to a double bind, for women are criticized by each other and by viewers if too financially dependent on a husband but also if too ambitious in their own career. A similar double standard applies in dating shows like *The Bachelor/ Bachelorette*, where women are criticized if too focused on their career but men don't suffer such censure (Dubrofsky 2014). This is in the larger context of much popular entertainment where career-oriented women are often knocked down and taught a lesson about caring for others and not being too assertive or personally ambitious. On RTV, sanctioned career choices for women are in appearance and image industries (clothing, hair, modeling, jewelry, cosmetics, interior design) and their most celebrated skills are in traditional home arts (decorating, clothing, cooking, entertaining). Even in other business realms, as in *The Apprentice*, there is commercially sanctioned sexism: attractive women use their sex appeal for business purposes, as encouraged by Donald Trump, who is even more embarrassing in his assessment of women's "assets" than the gruffer Alan Sugar. Meanwhile, the cartoon-ish mind/body stereotypes of *Beauty and the Geek* are still being reproduced, e.g. in an Australian version (2009–) also currently being broadcast in Britain.

Gender and consumption

Gender differences are also displayed through consumption habits and I suggest that on reality TV these codes often define contrasts between *interiority* and *exteriority*, *biological* versus *technical functionality*, and *personal* versus *public history*. Looking at con-sumer agency and social ambition also yields significant gender-specific patterns. Women's consumption is commonly depicted as interior and biological in the sense of being focused on self-image and personal appearance. The ultimate effect is for women to turn themselves and particularly their bodies into commodities, espe-cially when they elect to have cosmetic surgery (much has been written about this).[8] Surgery represents the attempt to construct gender by literally shaping the body according to scripts circulated by culture, or specifically media advertising. When they appear on TV makeovers, the previously unmediated become fulfilled not just by being mediated but by being mediatized, meaning conform-ing to media images.

As already noted, a highly feminized ritual of body display that appears in several reality formats is the wedding. With brides we see an infatuation with goods accorded a deep symbolic meaning and the affective substitution of goods for people (dress as love object and groom as prop). The two most entrenched scenarios today's RTV brides covet are the fairy-tale ending and the celebrity event. Both are conceits largely created by the media, both promise a temporary elevation of status, and both require big spending. Having one's wedding appear on TV usually achieves one or both of these aims. Across several TV formats extreme spending is cur-rently enacted mostly by women (lavish docusoaps, compulsive hoarding, big weddings) and extreme (risky or difficult) earning is mastered by men (as in *Deadliest Catch* or *Gold Rush*). Only the latter has the potential to be heroic.

Whereas feminine series focus on relationships that are in part built on consumer events, masculine formats typically focus on topic and activity (trading, hunting, customizing) that are then *supplemented with affect*. Female consumers generally express a high opinion of their worth but require lots of attention and social validation. When men consume it often builds and extends their *outer-directed sense* of power and domain. RTV portrays masculine consumers as interested in objects that allow them to interact with, and alter, the exterior physical world. Their interest is directed outward and rarely inwards, on their body. What they purchase is more inclined to deflect attention away from themselves on to grander and predominantly masculine achievements such as historical or industrial prowess. Whereas retail shopping of all kinds is generally coded as feminine or gay, the more masculine activities of trading and collecting are validated because they are portrayed as having a broad educational, historical, or patriotic significance. The more autonomous male subjects undergo different, self-initiated rituals (hunting, negotiating, aggressive competition) and pursue different kinds of objects (cars, weapons, tools). If they buy things (as distinct from shopping) they typically do so professionally and in order to generate a profit. This is the macho ideal, anyway, for there are variations for gay men and more metrosexual types. Macho consumers are depicted as competitive warriors on formats with titles like *Auction Hunters* (Spike 2010–) or *Storage Wars*. They negotiate and take risks. This is explicit in the Las Vegas-based *Pawn Stars* which reminds us that gambling is at the base of much commerce: negotiation relies on poker faces, keeping cards close to the chest, and taking chances. Or, like frontiersmen, these individuals travel through a largely uncharted territory where prices are not fixed and have to be assessed on the fly. This requires quick and decisive action, as well as courage, skill, and a somewhat combative attitude. Even muscular force is useful when scaling piles of objects, hauling out hidden treasures, or arm-wrestling to settle on a price; all of which turns genteel antiquing into a rugged sport. What Rick, the Bruce Springsteen lookalike on *American Restoration*, restores is both national and masculine pride. He and other male consumers express a nostalgic reverence for American manufacturing, brands like Harley-Davidson, Remington, Colt, machines made by men for men. The implication, certainly on the History channel, is that history, too, is made by men, owned by men, and can be traded in the form of commodities.

Bodies

As elsewhere on TV, many RTV figures are above average in looks, whether in docusoaps where appearance is an obsession, in gamedocs where most are young and fit, or even in home improvement formats where building contractors resemble (and indeed have been) advertising models. But the more ordinary or even unattractive have their uses too. They are problem figures like hoarders or the abnormally overweight or out of shape, whether regenerate (makeover subjects) or unregenerate (rednecks, chavs). Some talent shows take pride in advancing relatively unattractive singers, but still the trend is for the physically attractive to have most success – which is, of course, a realistic reflection of the music or entertainment business.

So much RTV programming is about sexualized bodies: "housewives" perform on stripper poles, kids vamp in pageants, half-naked adults writhe on *Dancing with the Stars*, while representatives of the actual porn industry are normalized as the *Girls Next Door* (E! 2005–10). Indeed, reality TV is part of a larger trend of mainstreaming of what was previously considered illicit – i.e., pornography. Women strip (usually not professionally) and men, too, display their physical assets as dates or gigolos. Some shows capitalize on society's premature sexualization of children: as a result, one father used his wife's dressing of their daughter as a prostitute on *Toddlers and Tiaras* to win child custody.

RTV is also at the forefront of the mainstreaming of cosmetic surgery, now a booming area of medicine. The PR for this kind of alteration in countless makeovers and docusoaps may be one of the most striking examples of television making a real socio-economic impact. Its exact influence is hard to determine, but this programming has certainly coincided with the biggest increase in patients and best public relations in the history of cosmetic surgery, a branch of medicine not always held in high regard. TV surgeons have seen a tremendous increase in their business and many patients report that viewing reality TV motivated them to have a procedure (Crockett et al. 2007: 323).[9] Foregrounded in some series or normalized as a regular element in others, having "work done" is represented as something people with any discretionary spending now engage in to boost their market value. Even for the less affluent, charitable makeovers suggest that cosmetic procedures are not indulgent or vain but deserved and therapeutic. In both instances, TV's publicizing of procedures appears to have removed shame: now plastic surgery is often depicted as a sign of empowerment, as the surest way to boost self-esteem and achieve self-improvement. It is also an individual choice – with no consideration of the systemic reasons why someone would opt for it.[10] There is on RTV little pretense at psychiatric counsel and no suggestion that anyone should criticize or reform the social attitudes that have created the desire. There is also, of course, no acknowledgment that television has had a part to play. Yet its daily procession of ideal images – images that are often possible only in mediation (digital alteration) – is used, first, to attract viewers (because beauty attracts) and, second, as goals viewers are encouraged to meet through purchases of advertised goods and services. In this way television feeds the beauty industry and vice versa. RTV reflects that, thanks to surgery, beauty is a commodity, a prize, or gift (from husband to wife or mother to daughter). For many RTV subjects, electing to have surgery is framed as an opportunistic, postfeminist working within the system, where the body is a source of power through sexual objectification (Gill 2007; Tasker and Negra 2007).

Whether surgery is ever truly empowering or the opposite is a debate that some RTV series have brought to the fore. Feminist scholars generally condemn the uptake of cosmetic surgery as succumbing to patriarchal notions of a woman's worth, putting too much emphasis on physical attractiveness and robbing women of genuine agency and self-esteem (e.g., Bordo 1993; Banet-Weiser and Portwood-Stacer 2006: 263). Kathy Davis (2003), however,

argues that electing for surgery can be a rational response to patriarchal and capitalist constraints and suggests that most patients
simply wish to be taken as normal: indeed, we often hear on TV
makeovers this desire to "fit in." But numerous media effects
studies have suggested that one of television's strongest effects is to
alter what viewers regard as normal and raise the beauty standards
that viewers feel obliged to reach, with consequent mental and
physical ill-effects.[11] The template is not, therefore, the statistically
average but the media-worthy. Certainly TV surgeons and clients
interpret "feminine" not as an average middle-aged body but as
someone attractive for being in their sexual youth (flat stomachs,
taut breasts): indeed, it seems even women with babies have to be
sexy as part of a status-driven lifestyle (*Pregnant in Heels*, Bravo
2011–).[12] Makeovers reinforce the commercial push to make a
natural process – aging – into a problem that needs fixing. It is
fixed by buying products that promise to close a perceived (and
highly profitable) gap between ideal image and reality. In addition, from a media economy perspective, TV's normative display
of attractive young bodies not only attracts attention but also
matches a coveted youth demographic.

There is not space here to properly engage in a debate about
whether body alteration is a matter of victimhood or agency. Some
scholars maintain that even when an individual feels that surgery
is liberating, "In fact, what is happening is a more intense polic-
ing of the body" (Banet-Weiser and Portwood-Stacer 2006: 263).
Others argue that, for any individual, the option may be empowering and rational given the sociopolitical conditions under which
she acts (e.g., Davis 2003). Many scholars identify both empowerment and oppression (e.g., M. Jones 2008; Morgan 2009: 70–2)
and are unwilling to dismiss patients as simply deluded or vain.
Certainly, it would be naïve to declare these TV programs mis-
taken when they suggest that personal appearance affects how
people regard each other or themselves – or that these two attitudes are interrelated. But RTV producers are not interested in
in-depth back stories or expensive longitudinal studies that might
reveal larger sociopolitical forces. As with much reality TV, *the
intimacy is superficial*. Viewers are given snapshots of lives that

inspire empathy and short circuit politicization, ratifying instead the pseudo-individualism of the advertising that supports them.[13] Once again, commercial pressure curtails sociopolitical content.

Sexual orientation

RTV has been significant in relation to gay identity, given that its representations of this sexual minority were early and frequent. But of course an increase in cultural visibility doesn't necessarily mean an increase in understanding or complexity (Gamson 2014). Some claim that reality TV was the vehicle for the first coming out of a gay man on TV, with Lance Loud on *An American Family* in 1973, but actually his family already knew and there was no explicit discussion of his sexual orientation in the series. Years later, fairly reliable drama was created by regularly juxtaposing gay and homophobic characters on MTV's *The Real World*, one of the few media locations where gayness and prejudice were openly discussed. *Real World*'s gay cast members continue to not only induce confessional revelations and spark drama but also allow producers to congratulate themselves for teaching tolerance. Another approach to representing gay-straight relations emerged with *Queer Eye* (2003), a series that got plenty of attention from viewers and media critics alike and even briefly appeared on network TV. Here gay men are fun, charming, and have come out in order to improve other people's closets – a comic turn that has provoked debate in scholarly and journalistic quarters about whether this series reinforced or broke stereotypes and the degree to which it supported heteronormativity.[14] Some characterized the series as a form of gay minstrelsy, where a few narrow stereotypes were trotted out for the amusement of a heterosexual audience (Sawyer, quoted in Sender 2006: 133). Joshua Gamson (2014) and others have observed that on RTV gayness is more often a consumer identity than a political one. So to the extent that they promote consumerism and style gay men are validated – but not much further.

From *Queer Eye* on, RTV has played a prominent role in main-streaming gay characters on TV and in recent years, gay (male) identity has become fairly unremarkable on a range of shows, particularly those produced by openly gay executive producer Andy Cohen for Bravo TV; Cohen, in his meta-shows like reunions and *Watch What Happens*, himself frequently discusses gayness and prejudice. In recent years when this mainstreaming is reversed, controversy can arise. For example, *Chrisley Knows Best* (USA Network 2014) generated controversy because many viewers felt the father was denying his real gay identity, an apparent disconnect that either irritates or amuses but certainly attracts attention. Meanwhile the patriarch of *Duck Dynasty* (A&E 2012–) was briefly suspended by the broadcaster after making anti-gay remarks (December 2013). This response to an off-the-air magazine interview indicates how unacceptable such sentiments have become. It also reinforces that an RTV participant is an employee and RTV a privately owned "public" forum.

RTV's gay males usually appear in stereotypical areas of cultural production. They can be experts on wedding and style shows or judges on competitions about fashion or food. They do not appear on formats featuring hunting or manual labor. Whereas some protagonists' sexual identity is muted or undeclared, many more perform very self-consciously. Yet there is generally little interior view of their personal life, so the embrace is still tentative. Many figure as best friends or assistants who add some cachet to the privileged nouveaux riches. A few series refer to painful coming out memories but in most scenarios any difficulties or prejudices are largely glossed over. At the time of writing, gays are still absent from mainstream network romance/mating shows. But even rarer on RTV or elsewhere in the media are lesbian characters. One exception was the gym owner on *Work Out* (Bravo 2006) and years later the highly glamorized and sexualized *The Real L Word* (Showtime 2010–12) where, as Dana Heller despairingly notes (2014), commercially driven fantasies reflected nothing of the authentic political and collective experiences of most lesbian women. More down-to-earth is the ensemble character Rosie, the brusque but beloved cousin on *The Real Housewives of New Jersey*, or ordinary viewers watching TV on *Gogglebox*. Gay, and again more rarely lesbian, contestants are also part of the mix on talent competitions, docusoaps, and gamedocs like *Project Runway* or *Top Chef*, series that are congratulated for not making gays exceptional or token: in 2007 *Project Runway* was nominated for a GLAAD (Gay & Lesbian Alliance Against Defamation) award for its inclusive representation. Gay participants also regularly appear on major network ensemble series like *Big Brother*: some prominent examples in Britain were *Big Brother 2* winner Brian Dowling, a runner-up lesbian ex-nun Anna Nolan, and the even rarer transsexual figure of Nadia, winner of series five (2004). These significant comings out for the British public were mostly warmly received (interestingly all three are foreign nationals). Not so well-liked was Richard Hatch, the scheming first winner of America's *Survivor*, who went on to serve time in prison for tax evasion. Gay identity has also been thematized on fairly minor series like *Boy Meets Boy* (Bravo 2003), while drag queens take center stage on *RuPaul's Drag Race* on the LGBT channel Logo (2009–). A gay couple emerged as central in *Flipping Out*, and *Newlyweds: The First Year* (Bravo 2013) underscored that a gay couple can now perform as one example of marriage. However, none of these figures inspire a wider sociopolitical debate or go beyond individual circumstances within the broadcast texts.

Most gay characters on RTV seem fairly sanguine, though a few acknowledge suffering trauma. On *The Shahs of Sunset* (Bravo 2012–) a gay protagonist repeats how he'd be killed in his Iranian homeland and is barely accepted by his immediate family in the US, yet he generally maintains a positive sub-tragic demeanor. In many series, gay men appear to be appreciated for their entertainment value and are most useful to producers if flamboyant, volatile, and upbeat. On *Queer Eye*, as is often pointed out, the presenters performed as self-confident and largely unapologetic gay men but their ultimate purpose was to serve heteronormativity and institutions such as marriage from which they were banned: their own private lives, their own rights or challenges, were invisible. All of the Fab Five projected the flamboyant stereotype for whom being gay was a fun lifestyle – thus potentially playing into conservative prejudices (Miller 2006: 115). In more recent shows there is a greater variety of personae, including more reserved authority figures like Tim Gunn, the generous mentor on *Project Runway*.

Race

If we assume that race is still a category in current use, we can ask: How diverse are the representations of race? What kinds of stereotypes appear and have these modified over time? Should the subject being cast to represent a certain race bear any responsibility for playing a stereotypical role, especially if they purport to be representing a real person? Do producers have any obligation to present fair and unbiased portraits? Some of these questions are difficult to answer, especially the latter, and I want to start by recommending the approach of, for example, Shohat and Stam (1994) who dismiss as wrongheaded a "corrective approach" that simply looks for *errors* in the representations of raced identities and assumes that an accurate or true representation can be known and insisted upon. Content analysis can record frequency of representation and compare this to population demographics. Stereotypical portraits, too, can be fairly easily identified. But determining what constitutes a fair or realistic or appropriate representation is complex and cannot rely on a universal standard of truth or even verisimilitude. An assessment of representation (including stereotypes) must consider, among other things, viewer interpretation, genre conventions, and target audience. Furthermore, commentators can't simply separate stereotype and authenticity and isolate one from the other. Both in the media and in everyday life conventions and expectations shape behavior, so performing too far from what is expected can be read as lacking truth and authenticity can be a matter of performance. In addition, any representation entails selection and therefore the likelihood of partiality and even distortion, so the question becomes *what* does reality TV select and (where possible) *why*? My attempt below to address these questions is based mostly on American programming and to a lesser extent British portrayals.[15]

Most scholars agree that media representations of race matter due to both external and internal processes: unlike gender, media portraits might be the only glimpse some people have into lives of people with a different identity, and when the racial group depicted sees how it is perceived by others, individuals can subsequently internalize and/or resist. If this is its impact then it can be insidious, given that racial identification is largely a visual matter and TV portrayals can influence notions of race without overt discussion. Quantitatively, televisual representations have never precisely reflected real-life population percentages and some underrepresented minorities have a greater proportional representation than others; for example, currently US Blacks over Latinos. Reality TV is no exception. Some applaud this programming for being more racially diverse and integrated than other types of programming – and again *The Real World* led the way in this regard – but it is important to look at *how* people are being selected and portrayed. It is not sufficient to simply head count or even organize entries into positive or negative columns. Attitudes to race are multidimensional and negotiated, in this case between producers, participants, and viewers.

Although supposedly based on selected common physical characteristics resulting from genetic ancestry, race, most scholars today uphold, is more a social than a biological distinction or certainly a combination of both. While nineteenth-century White Europeans were confident in making charts indicating definite racial borders, scientific studies today suggest that genetic markers are weak. Indeed, some would go so far as to say that asserting definitive race categorizes is the root of racism, that categorization denotes and enacts discrimination. Still, for the sake of brevity and to reflect popular discourse, I employ conventional labels such as "Black" (African) or "White" (European, Caucasian) – even though things are (as they say) not just black and white. In both American and British media, non-Whites are identified racially but Whites generally are not. Anglo-American RTV is predominantly produced by, and features, White people and its producers tend to *commodify other races as sources of entertainment*, as something that adds color so to speak. So to the extent that underrepresented races have a novelty factor or voyeuristic appeal, diversity has a market value. Most contemporary TV (other than stand-up comedy) avoids overt expressions of racism even as a satiric technique (cf. 1970s sitcoms like *Till Death Us Do Part* or *All in the Family*): the orthodoxy is that all individuals are, or should be, firmly against it. But RTV programming is significant for the way it displays and critiques racism, sometimes head on. Race or racism is at least an occasional talking point on a variety of popular series such as *The Real Housewives*, *America's Top Model*, *The Kardashians*, and *Dance Moms*. That RTV foregrounds social categories as performances also has the broader potential to critique racism and other forms of discrimination.

Some programming purports to exist in a postracial environment in which participants protest loudly that they are "color blind." Meanwhile, much sought-after drama can be attributed to an airing of racial prejudices and the reproduction of standard repertoires and stock characters, with perhaps an unusual emphasis on RTV on newly rich Blacks. So far, allowing ordinary people to play themselves does not appear to have resulted in more complex or nuanced depictions of race: see, for example, Andrejevic and Colby (2006) on the limits of this participatory promise.

Models of racial incorporation

As elsewhere in the media, the majority of reality shows display a hegemonic and uninterrogated Whiteness, while the presence of other races takes on different forms. In what we might call *muted* representations, people of color are present in ways that don't draw attention to this identity, a form of the "positive realism" advocated by pioneering African American advertiser Thomas Burrell to describe putting unmarked people of color into dignified, everyday situations. For instance, *Ice Loves Coco* (E! 2011–13) features a mixed race couple but, while their differences are visually strong, their racial identities are not usually commented upon. In *variegated* situations, non-Whites are often part of the mix, as on predominantly White gamedocs, makeovers, and talent shows. They are also part of, but not serious contenders in, relationship series like *The Bachelor*.[16] These shows treat issues of race only obliquely. If they refer to race at all, as in some makeovers, then racial features are treated largely as a style issue and surgeons just "refine" African noses or Asian eyes (B. Weber 2009: 135). The mix of racial identities appears to be a tokenism intended to look pluralistic but is likely more a product of market research than ideology and not a true expression of different voices (Hasinoff 2008: 330). These are assimilationist programs (H. Gray 1995), where people of color are integrated into a majority White world with few links to their own culture or to larger structural inequalities. Here presence doesn't necessarily mean power. So much has this ultimately effacing tokenism become a cliché that in the parody *The Joe Schmo Show* actors were explicitly labeled as: "the big muscular token Black guy that appears on reality shows," "the over-achieving Asian," and a Latino called Chico who is a charming ex-con.

In less common *foregrounded* representations, racial differences are a central focus and are treated as the defining feature of someone's identity; as, for example, in some episodes of *Wife Swap*, *Top Model*, or a rare series like *Black. White.* (FX 2006). Praised by some for at least addressing racism, *Black. White.* families put on makeup to disguise themselves as the other's race. Not surprisingly this attracted criticism for suggesting that such a superficial change would allow someone to truly inhabit another racial identity.[17] *Survivor: Cook Islands* (2006) also somewhat controversially separated participants according to race (African, Asian, Latino, and White) and while some saw this racial segregation as too close to painful episodes in American history, others argued that it shouldn't be any more controversial than dividing by gender. Producers simply argued that it gave more spots to non-White contestants.[18] Actually, as a social experiment it fell flat and was not able to develop much insight. Nevertheless, this series was a good example of the burden of representation when members of the non-White tribes expressed their desire to give a good impression and dispel some myths about their racial group. Synecdochally, they became examples of a whole and were overcharged with allegorical meaning (Shohat and Stam 1994: 208).

When *Survivor* tribalized Whites and *Black. White.* put Blacks in whiteface, both shows marked Whiteness in a way rarely found in popular culture. Similarly, on *America's Next Top Model*, Black models were made up to look like Whites and Whites like Blacks, though it is not at all clear why this would be part of a model's training. This series, headed by an African American host, does regularly raise race as an aesthetic and commercial concern. Generally Tyra Banks is careful not to favor one race over another and both Black and White models have emerged as winners. However, having contestants imitate another race is, again, easily criticized as trivializing racial identity. If this race-bending was intended as a more sophisticated deconstruction of the arbitrariness of racial categorization, then this potential is not articulated in a show that seems content to play dress up. *Top Model* shows, in fact, how racial identity as a visual matter can be marketed and commodified (Hasinoff 2008; Squires 2014). Generally non-White appearances are sold as exotic and we also see here, as elsewhere, an infra-racial colorism that favors more Caucasian features on African bodies (lighter skin, straighter hair), although in other series (e.g., *The Real Housewives of Atlanta*) we are beginning to see some push back, with for example pride in a prominent (assumed African) "butt." *The Real World*, by pitting rural Whites with unthinking racist views against urban Blacks, has for years suggested that racism is an individual problem attributable to ignorance and a sheltered existence and so can be fixed through friendship and education: the problem is biographical not political. Viewers therefore get to feel above racism while the real structural determinants remain largely unexamined (e.g., Kraszewski 2004). Another form of depoliticization is when viewers get to feel that some charges of racism are trumped up: as in the notorious case of Omarosa, a Black contestant on *The Apprentice* who was perceived to use false accusations of racism as a strategy to protect herself as victim, generating much furor online and elsewhere.

Occasionally there are all-Black or dominant Black casts on American reality TV that are pluralist or separate-but-equal (H. Gray 1995): among them, Bravo's nouveau riche *The Real Housewives of Atlanta*, *Married to Medicine* (2013–), and *Thicker Than Water* (2013). Here Black experience is generally seen as parallel to that of Whites and there is little attention to racism, racial inequality, or to diversity or tensions within Black culture. If individuals struggled on the way up, we don't hear much about it. Viewers could infer that these shows reflect a postracist as well as neoliberal America: both terms emphasizing individualism over collective identity. Or maybe class/money simply trumps race, for subjects and for viewers (Smith 2008). Several casts feature African Americans – often newly wealthy due to prowess in sports or entertainment – who largely follow the conventions of Whites in the same tax bracket but who switch into a self-conscious urban Black dialect as a way of bonding or of "keeping it real," meaning true to lower-class roots. However, they just as freely use terms like "ghetto" as a derogatory slur. Even more rare are Black-produced reality shows, usually found on BET (Black Entertainment Television), a channel with relatively little original programming: RTV examples are *College Hill* (2006–), *Baldwin Hills* (2007–9), *Harlem Heights* (2009) and *The Family Crews* (2010–11). However, the real ratings juggernaut remains Bravo's *The Real Housewives of Atlanta*.

Racial stereotypes

Stereotyping isn't about mistakes or inaccuracy: it is closer to culpable simplification. Who is stereotyped reflects, in part, a larger power hierarchy that determines who matters or is worth knowing or paying attention to. On TV, stock characters also reflect the needs of entertainment. On RTV, African Americans are portrayed differently to some extent according to gender, with more focus to date on the drama generated by women – likely because they project the largest and loudest emotional performance. As well as being sexualized, most of these women are loud, brash, vulgar, belligerent, and argumentative, although some can be seen more positively as entrepreneurial, energetic, or candid. Black men tend to have a different bodily presence. In some instances they provide an edge: they are seen as dangerous, angry, violent, or sexually aggressive, as often on *The Real World* (Orbe et al. 2001; Kraszewski 2004; Bell-Jordan 2008). Or on gamedocs they may be regarded as lazy, quarrelsome, unreliable, but also strong (Wright 2006). On more recent female-driven docusoaps the men are more muted. They may assert patriarchal privileges and occasionally get into physical altercations (as do some women), but their wives tend to overshadow them and many husbands appear ineffectual except as peacemakers between feuding women. Indeed, some divorce when eclipsed by their wives' growing income and celebrity. A few African American men appear as judges or experts (e.g., talent shows) and occasionally as credentialed professionals (e.g., doctors), but archetypal examples of strong and valid masculinity currently show up in the form of White male indoor or outdoor entrepreneurs. Black males tend to be more urban and domestic (domesticated?). Or they appear as criminals (inmates, car thieves), and so a threatening but largely contained underclass (*Cops*). For many, a particularly egregious portrait of Black masculinity was *Flavor of Love* (VH1 2006–8), one of the first predominantly Black casts with a Black protagonist and popular among Black viewers. Critics decried it as a horribly demeaning and sexist show that reflected badly on Black culture. The scrawny and arrogant protagonist, rapper Flavor Flav, also appeared to be self-consciously ridiculous and clownish and so some commentators regard the series as a twenty-first-century minstrel show.

Perhaps even more cringeworthy, and certainly more prevalent, is RTV's Angry Black Woman (Pozner 2010: 166), especially the inarticulate and physically aggressive "Sista With an Attitude (SWA)," an eye-rolling, finger-wagging RTV staple who perceives personal and racial slights everywhere. Not so much powerful as pushy, these women often combine two categories: the promiscuous, vacuous jezebel and the grasping, arrogant diva. Both are akin to the exhibitionist and self-deluded buffoons who have long been used to entertain majority-White audiences. Their vulgar behavior helps give the impression that "all the money in the world couldn't make rich Black women civilized" (Pozner 2010: 186) and they are quick to denigrate fellow strivers as "boudgie" or "uppity." Only an occasional (and non-mainstream) BET series offers a glimpse into the lives of well-mannered, upper-middle-class Black families who respectfully discuss serious matters and whose daughters wear purity rings (*Baldwin Hills*). Images of upwardly mobile Blacks are not new on American TV, but compared to the earnest and hardworking characters of 1970s and 1980s sitcoms (*The Jeffersons*, CBS 1975–85) and the sophisticated Huxtables (*The Cosby Show*, NBC 1984–92), today's RTV families are more often shallow, brash, and lacking in cultural capital. This becomes particularly significant for the synecdochal weight it bears, a burden not placed on badly behaved Whites.

In America, people of African descent are the most commonly represented people of color, presumably because for some time (but no longer) they have been the largest racial minority.[19] Britain's different imperial past means that its largest racial minority is of South Asian descent, predominantly Indian and Pakistani. Since the 1980s, British media regulators have explicitly encouraged multiculturalism but it is still rare to have an all-Black or even predominantly Black TV cast.[20] As in the US, Black participants appear as part of the mix on ensemble casts and in gamedocs or talent shows. A somewhat limited Africa Channel (2007) features African news and entertainment, some programs developed in Britain and others imported from Africa. But for some years people of African descent have so rarely been seen in central or authoritative positions anywhere on TV that the highly assimilated newscaster Trevor McDonald was a notable exception and comedian Lenny Henry seemed almost the sole representative of Black entertainers (indeed, he has been campaigning for years for more minority representation). Meanwhile blackface is still being used by Sacha Baron Cohen as rapper Ali G – albeit to flush out and skewer racist attitudes.

Other races and ethnicities

Asians (Chinese, Japanese, Koreans, Vietnamese) are frequently depicted in American media as unemotional, intelligent, technical, humorless (Wang 2010) and, if successful, overly disciplined and without creativity or individuality. When Asian Americans occasionally appear on RTV some of this stereotype melts a bit. Some on career shows like *Top Chef* and *Project Runway* are seen as creative and emotional, though even here their expertise tends to be in technical skills rather than passion. Fewer succeed in entertainment formats like talent shows, the notoriously bad *Idol* audition by William Hung only preserving the stereotype of the Asian geek. In Britain, people of Indian and Pakistani descent are a stronger media presence. As a deliberate policy to encourage multiculturalism, some magazine programs have been produced by and for South Asians and, in a self-selected segregation, some British viewers access Asian-produced programming via satellite. A few sitcoms have centered on Indian British characters, such as *Goodness Gracious Me* (BBC2 1998–2001) and *The Kumars at No. 42* (BBC2 2001–6), these satirizing both Anglo and Indian cultures. Films like *My Beautiful Launderette* (1985) or *Bend it Like Beckham* (2002) also occasionally raise the profile of Asian Britons. But media representation is sparse. Regarding RTV, one iteration of the RTV series *The Family* (2009) featured an Indian British family (Malik 2012) and in 2010 a Nigerian British family. Asian identity in a talent show format was focused on in *Bollywood Star* (C4 2004) and other British Asians have done well on shows like *Britain's Got Talent* (ITV 2007–).

Of course, the most notorious discussion of race and racism in Britain was provoked by incidents on the 2007 *Celebrity Big Brother* when remarks by Jade Goody and others to and about Bollywood actress Shilpa Shetty created a storm that led to thousands of viewer complaints, hundreds of newspaper articles, countless blog debates, official declarations from both the British and the Indian governments, street protests in India, the withdrawal of show sponsors, and finally the suspension of the program and mandatory apologies. The broadcaster Channel 4 had been set up to introduce more racial diversity into British broadcasting and so perceived racism on its most successful program soon became a high-profile case. The working-class Goody, who was popularly vilified and even received death threats, repeatedly apologized for her remarks and subsequently took part in the Indian version of *Big Brother* in 2008, until notice of her cervical cancer and death soon after, at which point many had apparently forgiven her earlier remarks.[21]

Other races appear infrequently on either side of the Atlantic. Also controversial was the reality series *All-American Muslim* (TLC 2011) featuring the everyday lives of Lebanese Americans. When a small group of Christian evangelicals expressed their displeasure at the normalizing of Muslims/Arabs (these are usually conflated) and, in their view, the masking of their inevitable ties to radicalism and terrorism, this was enough to scare off advertisers. The series was not renewed despite counter protests and boycotts. A few other Middle Eastern Muslims are featured in *The Shahs of Sunset* but these tend to self-identify as "Persian," presumably because this connotes a positive exoticism and an ancient civilization, whereas "Iranian" would point to their link to a hostile state. Also a good portion of those featured are Jewish, not Muslim, Iranians.

A particularly underrepresented group is the American Hispanic or Latino, both terms indicating Spanish-speaking people of multiple races or ethnicities. While Spanish-language channels in the US (Telemundo, Univision) produce their own reality programming, Latinos rarely appear on English-language programs. In RTV, there has been some sustained but not profound attention in *The Real Housewives of Miami* (Bravo 2011–), otherwise often mute Latino workers appear on home makeover construction sites or work as maids and gardeners. Zoila, the maid from Nicaragua, has become a comic fixture on *Flipping Out* where her subservience is subverted as much as it is insisted upon (her White boss, Jeff, is always threatening to fire her but he also buys her expensive gifts and seems to regard her as a substitute mother). *Washington Heights* (MTV 2013) was pioneering because it focused on Latinos, specifically Dominican Americans, and its creators were also Latino. However, it was criticized for not showing enough distinctive ethnicity or rituals and was dismissed by some for being too bland. Like Blacks, Latinos can fare well as entertainers in talent shows. They also appear as criminals or, more specifically, smugglers or illegal immigrants.

Among Euro-American identities, RTV has reaped much from Italian Americans, most famously when *Jersey Shore* promulgated a self-conscious (some would say fabricated) "guido" identity

– previously an ethnic slur meaning uneducated, working-class, and probably thuggish.[22] The cast's hedonistic and vulgar display outraged several Italian American organizations and legislators, including the governor of New Jersey who vetoed a tax incentive for the show. However, these portrayals of Italian Americans were not much more vulgar or less marked than the also popular *The Real Housewives of New Jersey*. More palatable and less ethnically colorful are the industrious Italian middle-class families seen on, for example, *Cake Boss*.

Conclusion

Once again, what is striking is how self-conscious are the social markers on reality TV: people generally know they are playing someone who is feminine or gay or Black. Lines are not scripted but social scripts are nevertheless played out, usually leaning heavily on stereotypical or exotic behavior – largely because this brings ratings success. RTV, like other media, doesn't simply or precisely reflect population demographics. Its extrovert perspective highlights and exploits differences in gender, sex, or race for entertainment purposes: to ignite conflict or to perform a sentimental assimilation or depoliticization. Perhaps because it often targets a youthful audience, RTV programming focuses on malleable or transitional identities and on individual enterprise. Sometimes it mainstreams what before was marginalized and so can be regarded as progressive for those who support greater cultural visibility for certain identities. But rarely is the portrayal deep or nuanced or complex.

6

Class

Media representations of class matter, in part, because *real-life* and *mediated experiences* are still to some extent distinct from each other. Hence, the media might be someone's only way to access the intimate lives of those who occupy a different social location. Moreover, many media scholars now believe that representations likely contribute to the creation of one's own class identity more than was recognized in earlier industrial/Marxist models of class formation. These portraits therefore deserve scrutiny, especially as they don't always map on to actual socio-economic conditions (for example, there is generally an over-representation of upper-middle-class characters on TV). Yet class today is the most neglected of the cultural studies trinity and is often passed over in favor of race and gender, despite having been at the fore of Cultural Studies when it emerged in Britain. Indeed, as bell hooks has observed: "race and gender can be used as screens to deflect attention away from the harsh realities [that] class politics exposes" (2000: 7).[1] While advocacy groups keep a close eye on media representations of race or gender, there isn't the same attention to representations of class.

The discussion of class will lead to a final chapter on RTV's political import. This is not to imply that class is necessarily more political than race or gender; however, one could argue that class is more directly an expression of the socioeconomics that are at the heart of politics when seen broadly as the social relations that determine the allocation of power and economic resources. It turns out that reality TV provides several provocative and explicit examples of class representation. While in many RTV series class is muted or evaded just as it is in other programming, in others it is unusually conspicuous and becomes a topic of conversation among participants and viewers. Of course, these TV depictions are influenced by a variety of factors: among them, the class identity or identities of those whom advertisers and hence TV producers wish to attract, the largely unexamined class identity of those who produce the programming, the perspectives and needs of those who finance TV production, and the classes of participants who will most reliably produce certain dramatic outcome – for example, only certain demographics will agree to appear on RTV and comply with its demands.

Not having space for any in-depth account of how class is currently conceived, I will trace the representations of class in both American and British programming according to some commonly acknowledged stratifications. There still isn't, in fact, a wealth of empirical research on class in either nation, and sociologists have produced a variety of competing or not entirely compatible theories. This is not surprising perhaps, since as Beverley Skeggs (2005) points out, class as a way of understanding social behavior is not pre-given but is always in production. The difficulty starts with terminology for there are not even standard definitions and, while there is some consensus about which factors determine class, scholars do not agree on their relative weighting: usually included are family background, education, occupation, income, wealth, manners, lifestyle. Meanwhile, disputes about method include the relative importance of quantitative or qualitative data gathering, the value of self-reporting, and the extent to which class can be understood in isolation from gender or race (L. Weber 2010). There is a reluctance among some academics to even refer to class because of a poststructuralist critique of essentialism and reductionism and a late-twentieth-century switch from class politics to identity politics (e.g., rights for women, gays, minorities).

Given that class is not a formal, legal concept, some scholars express doubts about whether it is even a viable category within more meritocratic systems and supposedly increased class mobility. In Britain both the Right (Thatcher) and the Left (New Labour) have promoted the image of a new classless society (Leggott and Hochscherf 2010) and American politicians rarely invoke any label other than "middle class:" this is in part because most Americans identify as middle class and have been encouraged to do so. Any discussion of class differences is regularly transposed by conservatives into accusations of "class warfare." Indeed, openly referring to class in popular discourse is variously regarded as impolite, regressive, or possibly communist and "unAmerican," this despite some more explicit references to numbers in recent years: to wealth disparity and to the 1 percent identified by the Occupy Wall Street movement in 2011.[2] In the US and UK "class unconsciousness" (Grindstaff 2011b: 202) can also be traced from the bottom up, from the post-industrial weakening of the labor movement and subsequent lack of collective identity, substituted by an individualist interpretation of the American Dream and Thatcher's promotion of a post-society neoliberalism (whence Norman Tebbit's advice to the unemployed to get on their bikes).[3] Neither culture is today comfortable with the word "poor," preferring bureaucratic terms like "low-income," "underprivileged," or just "ordinary people/folk." As we will see, recent RTV programming has found a way to skirt around this issue and use folksy and exotic substitutions for the poor or working class.

Most Anglo-American scholars agree on a minimum classification of upper, middle, and lower/working, with sometimes recognition of a non-working underclass. But class labels are not exactly cross-culturally equivalent: most notably, there are more nuanced distinctions within "the middle class" in British culture and pronounced differences between the professional upper-middle and the lower-middle class. In addition, how many classes or subclasses are distinguished would depend on the questions asked, the complexity of the society, and how fine-grained is the study. Some contemporary scholars prefer Max Weber's use of "status" in place of the fixed, exploitive, and antagonistic model of Marx, status being a more fluid category indicated by lifestyle, prestige, and popularity (social and cultural capital) rather than solely economic or occupational ranking. Status is regarded as more pertinent to post-industrial consumerist societies – and of course less liable to political analysis or collective action.[4] The transformative nature of much reality TV and its commercial impetus tend to emphasize status and social mobility (the makeover, the celebritization of unknowns).[5] Although recent programming also exploits the tensions found in a fixed social ranking.

To sum up so far: the concept of class today can be complicated or evaded because: (i) it is intellectually difficult to judge and affix ranks, or (ii) there are genuinely fewer fixed distinctions between ranks, or (iii) there is ideological pressure to evade or flatten distinctions even if they do exist. Then we have to consider the *perspectival nature* of class perceptions, the influence of one's own social position and broader national variants in judging class, and the difference between any objective academic scheme and how class is recognized by and made meaningful to social actors in everyday life. Of course, in the media economy it doesn't much matter if depictions allow different viewers to judge classed content differently so long as they watch the show. As a general activity, television watching has itself played a role in flattening class distinctions, since watching TV is one leisure habit shared by all classes. Though it appears to be more heavily viewed by the lower classes, its use is less class-inflected than music, visual art, or literature. Also one could argue that the entire media advertising industry promotes lifestyle over class as important to one's social identity. Regarding RTV specifically, audience studies suggest that there is little class variation among those who enjoy it but some studies report that aversion to this programming is particularly strong among the upper "professional-executive class" (Bennett et al. 2009: 138).

Class on reality TV

Entertainment programming generally avoids class articulation but RTV bucks this trend to some extent. It is not just that class identities are consciously performed but also that class is explicitly referenced by show participants and further discussed by viewers.

RTV producers use the fact that class is both an affective and ill-defined concept to provide viewers with impassioned but multiple viewing positions. As we know, a good deal of reality TV content is about judging the worth and character of other people and class becomes part of this assessment. When personal makeovers were in the ascendant (first half of the 2000s), it looked like much RTV programming reflected a broader inattention to class that is particularly marked in American culture. But more recently stereotypes and even caricatures have been trotted out to create easy comedy, mockery, or disgust. So if one element of neoliberal individualism is to deny class or at least reject its deterministic nature, this recent delving into fixed class differences works against this model.

RTV producers know how to capitalize upon issues about which people are curious but ill-informed and hence class has become another titillating topic. In modern times class is less visually marked than race or gender (Bourdieu's hexus notwithstanding) and RTV reveals some current confusion about this form of classification, especially in the US where class demarcations are less conscious and less explicit than in British programming and society. In the UK, class identity is often attached to a person's original cultural and social capital (often indicated by accent), whereas the American focus tends to be on current income, occupation, and lifestyle – but especially income. Unlike Gilded Age capitalists who aped the European aristocracy, it seems wealthy Americans are no longer keeping up with the Joneses (old East Coast polite society) but with the Kardashians (flashy big spenders). Yet some American RTV cast members and viewers are currently fascinated with who *has* or *does not have* "class" – as though it were a simple binarism. In American usage, having "class" or being "classy" is more a matter of performance and appearance than birth and background: though to use terms like "classy" usually signals that the speaker does not have any solid cultural capital. For many RTV viewers, class also has a dramaturgical dimension. On online forums they judge participants to "have class" if they do not appear to be acting or performing overmuch, or in such a way that masks their real-life personality, an attitude that *naturalizes class* and gives it an *ethical dimension*. Certainly, whatever their criteria, class designations create strong emotions like pride, humiliation, and disgust – the affective areas that RTV likes to provoke. Passionate viewer discussions reveal the current desire to gnaw away at class distinctions and, while some TV participants claim whatever class position they feel entitled to, this unmerited assumption aggravates many observers.

Reality TV explicitly raises questions like: How can you tell someone's class? What is the relation between money and class? How significant are origins and education? Is ethnicity a part of class stratification or outside it? Is marrying solely to boost one's status either socially or ethically acceptable? Can working-class identity be a matter of pride? That RTV features real people has several consequences: for instance, there are limits to which classes appear; class attribution can deeply insult and sting; and real people playing themselves may reduce producer liability and charges of being prejudiced or unfair. Because they are real people, participants may validate stereotypes – unless the viewer is savvy enough to factor in producer influence. Or, just as provocative, real people who display some level of performance might suggest how much class is a performance for all of us.

Class comes into play in RTV's portrayal of basic social behaviors such as domestic relations (dating, marriage, parenting) and other aspects of lifestyle (food, health, social rites, consumption patterns, leisure activities). It emerged as a theme early on when proto-reality series looked at families as class marked: the upper-middle-class *An American Family*, the working-class *The Family*, the nouveau riche *Sylvania Waters*. In the last decade, there has been some particular excitement about the nouveaux riches on luxury docusoaps and more recently a whole slew of shows about working-class people and their different forms of license and excess. More particularly, we see the inflection of class with regional or ethnic "color," a move that allows people to be openly mocked without raising charges of either class prejudice or racism. These *colorful/colored Whites* are seen as somewhat outside regular class hierarchies, but laughing at regional differences is a way to indirectly laugh at class inferiority. It suggests that a society officially vigilant about other forms of prejudice is apparently more tolerant of what is weakly referred to as classism: hence "classist" just doesn't have quite the stinging rebuke of "racist" or "sexist."

There are several ways in which class can become thematic. There may be a single focus on one class (often the extremes of rich or poor), though examining class with an overt policy or political agenda is rare (cf. Jamie Oliver). One class may be managing another (the makeover), or role-playing in titillating experiments with temporary poverty (*Tower Block of Commons*, C4 2010)[6] or the literal class tourism of *Holiday Hijack* (2011), where privileged tourists must slum it with natives. Some formats create a fish-out-of-water scenario (*The Simple Life*; *My Big Redneck Vacation*, CMT 2012-) or feature class mobility and class passing for lower-middle aspirants on makeovers, gamedocs, or ruses (e.g., *Faking It*, C4 2000-5; *Joe Millionaire*). Occasionally, game structures rely on class categories, as in *Kid Nation* (CBS 2007), where class switching was a central mechanism. Or they highlight class as a performance, as in *Masters and Servants* (C4 2003) or *What the Butler Saw* (C4 2004), where a family's imitation of aristocratic behavior is secretly being judged by their servants. Central to historical costume docusoaps is the reconstruction of class divisions that are blatantly harsh but also contained within a temporary pretense that is distanced through historicization (e.g., *Manor House*, C4 2002).

Working class

For some years British fictional programming has been more inclined than American TV to focus on working-class characters – from a predominantly middle and upper-middle class perspective. Early on were satires (*Till Death Us Do Part*, BBC1 1965–75) and quite sympathetic portraits (*Porridge*, BBC1 1974–7; *Boys From the Blackstuff*, BBC2 1980–2). There has also been a strong tradition of working-class evening soaps (the long-running *Coronation Street* or *EastEnders*) and class-themed historical dramas (*Upstairs, Downstairs* to *Downton Abbey*). One of the most popular sitcoms of all time, *Only Fools and Horses* (BBC1 1981–2003), was an affectionate (albeit ultimately patronizing) look at the upwardly mobile working class. However, in recent programming very negative views of the working class or under-class dominate: for example, *Shameless* (C4 2004–13), *Little Britain* (BBC 2003–6) and *The Royle Family* (BBC 1998–2000). In America there was some mocking of working-class prejudice and ignorance in *The Honeymooners* (CBS 1955–6), *All in the Family* (CBS 1971–9) and *The Beverly Hillbillies* (CBS 1962–71), then some sympathetic portraits from a working-class producer on *Rosanne* (ABC 1988–97). Soon after, *The Simpsons* (Fox 1989–), *Family Guy* (Fox 1999–2002, 2005–) and *My Name is Earl* (NBC 2005–9) reverted to the ineffective, especially male, buffoons, none of whom have the psychological complexity or aspiration to improve their lot. The main venue for working-class Americans outside fictional drama has therefore been talk shows and crime shows, neither of which produced many positive images.

RTV has, today, become a reliable way to make working-class identities productive for middle-class media producers and audiences, whether it be the good and deserving poor who need rescue (makeovers) or the badly behaved poor who are proud of their recalcitrance (numerous docusoaps). For some time RTV has exploited lower and lower-middle-class participants as cheap labor. Now their class position is being foregrounded and spectac-ularized. A flood of shows featuring rednecks and guidos (USA) or "chavs" and Essex people (UK) are now appearing on schedules. In a sort of careless *cultural fracking*, producers have been digging down and applying the considerable pressure of media expo-sure without much thought to social or political repercussions. Working-class characters are simply a cheaply mined resource, more easily lured by modest financial incentives and apparently less concerned about social embarrassment than those holding a superior status. In a kind of economic draft, many voluntarily participate even in humiliation: perhaps, as former RTV producer Laura Grindstaff suggests, because they feel socially marginal-ized and seek public attention (Grindstaff 2011a: 53). However, it is not clear what voluntary or consensual means if someone is acknowledged to have psychiatric problems (e.g., rehab shows, hoarders). While much documentary has been presented as serving the interests of the lower classes by earnest middle-class produc- ers, reality TV is clearly more open to charges of exploitation. For some time, and especially since the establishment of a welfare state, the working classes have been under bureaucratic surveil- lance, but here the probing is for entertainment purposes divorced from policy. In place of attempts at social reform, reality produc- ers seem content to harness limited and partial attitudes toward class identities simply in order to attract attention. The tendency is therefore to reinforce rather than challenge current class differ- entiation and to indulge in the kind of stereotyping that regulates social power. As Vicki Mayer's study of production practices discloses, producers don't just find people of a certain class but cast those who consciously or very obviously play this role (Mayer 2011b: 189). It is also likely that there is further class coaching. So the lower classes are allowed in on the producers' terms and, though they too may capitalize on the experience, it is clearly not an egalitarian arrangement.

There is, nevertheless, a range of attitudes to working-class participants: some portraits appear largely sympathetic (even if arguably misguided or patronizing), others more distant and neutral, and still others generate fear or disgust. There is a fairly consistent geographic bias where the bi-coastal (California/NYC) media industry enlivens fundamental American tropes such as the division between North and South (associating the defeated South with stupidity and lack of education). Britain conversely repro- duces from a southern/London base the marginalization of north- ern counties. The programming in both countries also reflects more global prejudices regarding rural vs. urban living or the strategy of attributing subordinate status to a subject's childish- ness and lack of discipline (of body and habitus) – a move that has historically linked patriarchy and colonization. Of course, there has been a long tradition of inflecting class distinctions with moral judgment and associating the lower classes with lower ethical standards, thereby justifying social inequality (e.g., Skeggs 2004;

Sayer 2005): this is captured in words that used to mean just *lower rank* such as villain (from the latin *villanus*, meaning peasant). The argument is that the poor do not succeed because they are lazy degenerates, feebleminded, untrustworthy, criminal, dirty – in fact both hygienically and morally unclean. Some of these portraits reappear as RTV entertainment where they are greeted by many viewers as a further debasement of society.

The lowest echelons on RTV are teen moms, minimum wage earners, debtors, and minor criminals. In Britain, there are some observations of grim under-class life on the geographic margins in *The Scheme* (BBC Scotland 2010–11) and *The Estate* (BBC N. Ireland 2012). These portray squalor, criminality, and desperation: some critics referring to them as voyeuristic "poverty porn." A controversial observation of the non-working class in *Benefits Street* (C4 2014) featured largely unmotivated people experiencing long-term unemployment, some of whom committed petty crimes. The series attracted both viewers and political debate, sparking parliamentary discussion of welfare policy and the exploitation of the poor for entertainment purposes.

There are, however, still some taboos. In neither nation do we see much about the long-term homeless or malnourished: a rare exception being the first *Real World* series when one roommate briefly befriended a homeless young woman. Certainly, within commercial media portraits of the completely abject would not serve an advertising-supported environment where the aim is to dangle goods before those who can afford them and their presence might ignite uncomfortable questions about the status quo. When there are glimpses of the underclass they are usually contained in law and order settings like *Cops*, where they are seen as immediately culpable and even comically stupid, but no one asks questions like why crime so often occurs in poor neighborhoods. More grim are various series set within the prison industry and the supposedly rehabilitative *Beyond Scared Straight* (A&E 2011–) which licenses yelling at the lower classes. We don't have to dwell on Foucault and the panopticon to understand how here TV has become part of a disciplinary regime. On teen pregnancy shows lower-class individuals demonstrate some of the largely negative repercussions of poor judgment/inadequate upbringing/lax morals, as was the case with the working-class *The Family*, where an unwedded teen pregnancy attracted plenty of public censure. Less morally culpable but starkly vulnerable are the surprised subjects on *Repo Games* (Spike 2011–) whose host offers to pay off their car debt if they correctly answer some trivia questions, or take their car away if they are incorrect. This preying upon people's financial difficulties and lower education levels for the entertainment of others begins to look very like class baiting.

If in any society it is believed that the middle class is expanding, then those who are still identifiable as lower class become a stigmatized "marginal rump" (Bennett et al. 2009: 177). This appears to be the case in Britain where the press has latched on to the term "chav" (surfaced c.2005) to indicate disgust at working-class figures who are presumed to be ignorant, sexually promiscuous, unemployable, and anti-social (O. Jones 2011). Like "yob," it comes out of a tabloid culture where right-wing-owned papers encourage lower-class readers to sneer at their own class (*The Sun*) or middle-class readers to express regular disgust (*The Daily Mail*). This was made very evident by the coverage of RTV star Jade Goody who as a celebrity chav became, in the eyes of a self-righteous middle class, emblematic of the many inadequacies of the working class.[7] Among working-class viewers it seems she garnered more empathy and sympathy (Wood and Skeggs 2011a).

One could argue that reality programming at least acknowledges that the lower class exists, but its shows are more popular than *populist* in the sense of representing the perspective and interests of ordinary people. Rather, caricatures of ordinary people are put on display because, without bourgeois discipline and inhibition (except of course as imposed by producers for filming purposes), they are almost guaranteed to deliver spectacularly inappropriate behavior and hence bankable ratings. So what we are witnessing is not a moral compunction to give voice to the underrepresented but *content diversity being driven by conservative and commercial goals*. Depictions of an abject lower class may also be tapping into a middle-class anxiety about, and fascination with, the degradation of society, a loss of civility, etc.

Class

For marginalized peers, there is presumably some interest in seeing those like themselves who are not ordinarily on TV. *The Family* (1974) was presented as allowing ordinary, working-class people access to the media as part of the BBC public service remit (Holmes 2008: 198). But for most viewers, who don't identify with those on screen, there is the schadenfreude of watching inferior others apparently proving their inferiority. While some online posts express envy (e.g., of license or freedom), and others ambivalence about those positioned at the bottom, most viewers vent exuberant class hatred as part of an expanding and engorging culture of sneering and derision – sometimes with a twist of casual affection – that links reality television to widespread amateur production on the likes of YouTube. There is an apparent tolerance for what Nick Couldry calls a downward directed "class abuse" (2011b: 34) where ordinary people are ridiculed, especially when they are (to invoke the fashionable paradox) so *bad* they are *good*.

Many of the lower classes on RTV are portrayed as too childish or debased to deserve better, or it is suggested that poverty is a choice, a voluntary or willful lifestyle. An apparent lack of interest in social mobility looks like self-imposed class limits and, while the internal homogeneity of these stereotyped groups allows them to function as recognizable brands, this does not seem to translate into political solidarity: certainly, if subjects have political affiliations we don't hear about it. Many individuals are portrayed as having fun and if they are at the same time being made fun *of*, it appears they don't mind or don't notice. Those who do notice seem to be performing a form of self-conscious self-condescension where, no doubt at the producers' prompting, they deliberately embrace negative stereotypes. Sometimes the mockery is direct and sanctioned, as with the pop-up commentary on "redneck" shows, but mostly viewers are encouraged to make their own appraisals – and, judging by online comments, they do.

Typically the mode is low comedy – i.e., physical, bawdy, farcical – a genre that since ancient times has employed lower-class characters as the comic butt, the drunkard, the buffoon. In particular, current RTV favors regionalized lower classes who are easily exoticized for market differentiation. For example, in the US and to a lesser extent the UK, accent diversity is shrinking in large part due to a predominantly middle-class, educated media production. But now it seems the media that eroded this diversification gets to mine what is left in the form of distinct regional and lower-class accents, whether Cajun or Boston or Geordie. In Britain, northern outposts like Manchester, Newcastle, and Liverpool have long provided conventionally subordinate others based on distance from the elite socio-economic institutions located in the South East (London, Oxbridge, and the "home counties" that surround London). For example, in *Geordie Finishing School for Girls* (BBC3 2011) four affluent young women from the south are transported to a poor neighborhood up north where the natives teach them the local dialect and rituals. Another transposition that could be seen as having hegemonic force is when working-class teens (plumbers, mechanics) are plopped into dire poverty in Africa or India in *Slum Survivor* (BBC3 2014) and report that they've learnt they should be grateful for what they have.

In America, producers tend to play up the humor and downplay more serious elements such as class-inflected racism or religious bigotry (e.g., the popular *Duck Dynasty* family is more religious and prejudiced than portrayed). They prefer members of the lower class who are having fun or (a different matter) strike others as funny. Subjects are portrayed mostly in their leisure activities and judged on their consumer habits, these being generally vulgar, childish, and hedonistic. Whether inhabitants of the Jersey shore or rural Louisiana, RTV's lower-class characters display little ambition or future goals: they live very decidedly in the moment (and likely plan their day as the producers prompt). The lighthearted *Redneck Rehab* (CMT 2012–) urges more socially elevated individuals to return to their redneck roots (beer, mud, hunting) and both *Bayou Billionaires* (CMT 2012) and *Duck Dynasty* celebrate how recent wealth doesn't change lower-class loyalties or behavior. The fact that they express pride in their culture may shield producers against charges of exploitation. Since participants are unapologetic, even proud, viewers may also feel entitled to condemn and to ridicule. Many online comments suggest that since they are cashing in on their TV appearance they are fair game.

Typically RTV viewers are given a decidedly exogenic (outside) perspective on amusing natives who ham it up in front of the camera in order to earn their keep. Even when TV success means some are quietly acquiring enough capital to move into a different economic position, they are still obliged to portray a lower-class lifestyle. Increasingly, producers concoct almost cartoonish scenarios that most viewers are meant to find ludicrous and rude – particularly the reasonably affluent middle classes whom broadcasters hope will attract advertisers. Here and elsewhere class prejudices are made palatable by painting lower-class figures as "colorful," marginal, and eccentric. These people come with subtitles. They are the *inner exotic*, the internally colonized. They are also part of a long tradition, from Greek comedy to Shakespeare, of containing the lower orders by making them into figures of fun.

The American redneck

As indicated, the specific category of the southern redneck has become a strong draw on recent American RTV. CMT (Country Music Television) in particular has enthusiastically developed the brand, launching several shows with redneck in the title. Other less explicitly named shows include *Duck Dynasty* and *Moonshiners* (Discovery 2011–). Several of these series have had decent ratings for cable shows, some occasionally beating network stalwarts like *Survivor* in key demographics (e.g., *Duck Dynasty*). Particularly controversial, however, was the launch of *Here Comes Honey Boo Boo* (TLC 2012–) which quickly became a lightning rod for derision and moral condemnation. Since at least the late nineteenth century, "redneck" has been used to designate poor, rural Whites, the descendants of sharecroppers whose neck was sunburnt from working outdoors. Today, "redneck" has become a self-consciously performed class persona (as recently revived by comedian Jeff Foxworthy and others), but those who wear this label are still somewhat defensive. Certainly "redneck" is less derogatory than the moral degeneracy and disapproval associated with urban "White Trash," a term first used by Black house slaves to denigrate landless

Whites in the 1830s and today used to express the discomfort other Whites feel at the uncanny presence of those who, despite being of the dominant race, are socio-economic and ethical failures. Being called White Trash is a deep insult among the nouveaux riches in *The Real Housewives*, where Aviva (*The Real Housewives of New York City*) explains that "What White Trash means is a moral failure." But whether redneck or White Trash, it is the association with lower-class status that makes Whiteness visible.[8]

In particular, rednecks embody two long-standing prejudices: against the poor per se and against the rural as being backward, ill-informed, and politically non-progressive. RTV tends to show "rednecks" as feral and edgy, outside the Marxist industrial context. In a form of homespun bricolage, they frequently repurpose and make do, turning road kill into a delicacy or a mud puddle into a fun park. These people improvise their material reality as part of their improvised drama, and it is up to the viewer to laugh at or admire their ingenuity, or both. But if they are admired by some for off-roading when it comes to mass consumption or social niceties, there appears to be a more unadulterated viewer condemnation when the poverty is of judgment, especially regarding parenting and diet. As is the case elsewhere, good and bad habits are marked according to restraint/excess and submission/license, the less reputable behavior being associated with the lower class. Take being overweight: this, in Bourdieu's terms, is an embodied cultural capital that often carries moral as well as class associations (laziness, lack of discipline, lack of proper upbringing) and RTV dwells on morbid examples of this, from *Honey We're Killing the Kids* to *Honey Boo Boo*.

A more innocuous but still enthusiastically attacked flaw is bad taste. Aesthetic preferences can depend on variables like age and gender, but on reality TV the firmest association is between lower-class rank and vulgar taste, a conventional social demarcation even in today's more omnivorous cultures. As with diet, the problem is excess. In bourgeois society, decorum generally requires moderation and restraint, but the logic of a lower-class aesthetics appears to be that if a few rhinestones look good, why not put as many as possible on any given item? If a poufy dress makes one a princess, then why not make it as big as a tent? Online viewer comments suggest there is something monstrous about lower-class attempts to make oneself seem important in this way, as when pageant children compete for overblown titles and elaborate plastic crowns. Yet some of this may be understood as a rational choice within a larger hegemonic structure: for being "queen" for the day or the "ultimate grand supreme" might well be a temporarily satisfying compensation for not having a high rank elsewhere.

In online discussion, some viewers appear to envy lower-class subjects when they don't seem to care what others think, an attitude that runs counter to so much other RTV programming. These figures represent the license to *not* improve, brushing off the more respectable judgments of those who, from nannies to nutritionists, elsewhere aim to upgrade their lower-class charges. This *non-interventionist* programming doesn't give viewers the excuse that participants, by being on these shows, are receiving help and that voyeurism is therefore productive. Many characters are simply meant to shock or offend middle-class viewers who are offered the opportunity to voice their contempt for the unashamed and irredeemable (*Bridezillas*; *Ibiza Uncovered*) – although some viewers express surprise that they like or even admire vulgar subjects, as when softened by comedy in the likes of *Honey Boo Boo*. Occasionally formats foreground class harmony and mutual respect, as in *My Big Redneck Vacation*, where lower-class fun and authenticity broaden the outlook of also stereotyped stuffy wealthy people. Some programs verge on a documentary-like attempt to understand and sympathize with a castigated lower class: as in the original British *Big Fat Gypsy Weddings* (C4 2010–12) which began as a one-hour documentary and when it became a hugely popular series still maintained some socio-political context and sober commentary. When imported into the US this quickly degenerated into silent mockery – although even the original title suggested a critical attitude to the behavior on display: "big fat" indicating ethnic and unsophisticated, after the film *My Big Fat Greek Wedding* (2002).

The redneck craze began just as the economy contracted in 2008, and this programming's pious pronouncements about family and friends being more important than anything else may be reassuring for those watching who don't have great financial security or success. Down-home redneck shows may also serve as an antidote to the faux lives of more nouveau riche characters, those with false smiles, false body parts, and false claims to wealth (although the redneck may be a role some deliberately play). Lower-class characters don't hide bodily functions and don't verbally euphemize, and so they come across as more authentic, or at least frank. But if popular shows raise awareness of class, they quickly diffuse its political charge when they frame those with few material resources as being happy with who they are. The ultimate validation of reality TV culture – being considered *authentic* – becomes *politically conservative* when it is accorded more worth than being wealthy, say, or powerful.

Some series rely on a high contrast between different classes – usually middle vs. working class – so the topic is foregrounded even if not explicitly labeled. Good examples are both British and American wife swap formats, or less pointed comparisons in *Come Dine With Me* (C4 2005–) and *Four Weddings* (Sky Living 2009–, TLC 2010–). Wife swap formats often feature a disciplined middle-class family versus a lazier and more excessive working-class family, but what is interesting is how often there appear to be strengths and limitations in both camps and it is up to the viewer to judge their relative merit (Wood and Skeggs 2011b: 95; Kavka 2012: 142). For instance, some participants push back on middle-class imposition and describe aspirant strivers as dupes. Many families agree to slight modifications but there is no real class agitation at the end, the majority being satisfied with the status quo.

Another strain in US programming displays some respect for working-class jobs if macho, stoic, and physically brave. This taps into a long-standing and particularly American fantasy about rugged independence. Primeval manual labor is romanticized and made adventurous,[9] unlike the antics of bumbling, indoor working-class sitcom figures. These outdoorsy mavericks are untamed and unsupervised. As modern frontiersmen (often in Alaska or some other wilderness) they represent entrepreneurial labor outside regular blue- or white-collar organizations. Their strength is centered in their body. There are also some sympathetic portrayals of skilled working-class jobs that involve pride in their craft by independent artisans, whether tattooing or car customization. Again, physical prowess is made meaningful.

Then there are the pathetic and deserving poor who appear in philanthropic formats like *Secret Millionaire* and *Undercover Boss*. In the latter, the conflicting needs of labor and capital are resolved in sentimental quest narratives and employer largesse. Innate inequalities are smoothed over and the status quo upheld, even revered. Foregrounded are examples of the good working class: plucky, valiant, uncomplaining service-economy workers who, almost to the point of masochism, go beyond required labor and swear company loyalty. There is no serious reform of working conditions and worker insight is frequently "rewarded" by the boss appropriating their ideas with no extra compensation. The latter invariably declares that "our people are our most valuable asset," which is presumably meant to gratify the loyal listeners by making them feel important but actually lays bare that they are indeed an exploited human capital.[10] What *Undercover Boss* thematizes, and much RTV production itself models, is the push for what economists call "increased productivity," which boils down to more labor for less pay. Numerous RTV shows involve tight deadlines, unrecompensed labor, and no overtime pay – both on and off screen. When they transform work pressures into a game and assemble teams (a popular management strategy), producers make stress entertaining and demonstrably effective, at least for those who succeed.

Middle class

On reality TV, this class is not only the middle but often the norm, and viewers are generally encouraged to identify with this, the demographic that advertisers seek and producers themselves identify with. Makeovers typically involve middle- or upper-middle-class experts advising lower-middle or working-class subjects.

(Although some hosts are ascribed different class identities by different commentators; for example, the British *What Not to Wear* hosts are labeled as everything from middle to upper class.[11]) Even when the expert is supposedly a computer, the machine has a crisp upper-middle-class accent on *Snog, Marry, Avoid?* (BBC3 2008–). Many scholars have noticed this normalizing of middle-class taste, especially in Britain.[12] Being middle class becomes an attitude, it seems, that anyone can and should adopt – thus de-anchoring class from socio-economic determinants. US presenters tend to use terms like "uptown" or "sophisticated" to describe the effects they create, again muting class coordinates: the casual suggestion is that class, privilege, and economic stratification can be fairly easily overcome. Sometimes the improvement format is more clearly seen as a class rescue, a popular subject on British television, from *The Fairy Jobmother* to *How the Other Half Live* (C4 2009–10) or *Millionaire's Mission* (C4 2007).

Generally the advice on RTV is in line with the middle-class values of order, discipline, and delayed gratification. Makeovers also reflect fairly affluent tastes and budget. No one goes into a middle-class home and makes it over into something working-class: Formica must be replaced by granite and plastic by steel. Only occasionally are there working-class experts and these are mostly in masculine realms (*Pimp My Ride*, *Dog Whisperer*, National Geographic 2004–11), where objects and pets are managed, not people.[13] However, viewer reaction to middle-class advice is not always positive. *What Not to Wear* hosts have been criticized by viewers for being rude and overbearing, and cultural scholar Angela McRobbie (2004) characterizes their denigration of lower-class women as a form of symbolic violence. Outside the power dynamics of the typical makeover there is also some admiration for stalwart lower-middle-class employees who go about their business in a service economy, usually with humor and good grace (*Airline*). Some, part of the US immigrant story, are small entrepreneurs who succeed on their own due to talent and hard work (business makeovers).

Nouveau riche

When it comes to locating high drama and subjects who provoke strong reactions, RTV producers have found more material among the nouveaux riches than earnest middle-class experts. These are the flashy, materialistic types, especially popular in America as non-fictional versions of its long-running glamorous soaps. Hugely, perhaps grotesquely, aspirant, these casts are both vulgar and wealthy and so many viewers are not sure whether to admire or loathe.[14] One appeal is, in fact, *wealth voyeurism*, a raw curiosity about how the other 1 percent lives. Although, as noted, it turns out that many RTV figures are actually nouveaux riches manqués who are over-reaching in order to *play* opulent consumers on TV: so in many instances the show creates the reality (luxurious lifestyles) that it purports to merely survey – not infrequently to the point of bankruptcy, or even death (suicide). Since the truly wealthy have little incentive to go on display, producers have to settle for an ersatz elite. Only a subset hungry for fame (Paris Hilton) or funds (Sarah, Duchess of York) will apply. This is the catch-22 of reality programming, that it would like to feature the elite but that anyone who would agree to participate is, by definition, not in this category. That is, reality TV *hits real limits in class representations* that fictional programming can ignore. Still, the nouveau subjects usually have a hugely inflated opinion of their social status and painfully little cultural capital with which to back it up, so the resulting dramatic irony is almost guaranteed to produce comedy, and sometimes unintended tragedy. When producers add in national or ethnic difference (e.g., *Ladies of London*, Bravo 2014–; *Meet The Russians*, Fox UK 2013–), there is further opportunity for distant mockery and tribal disdain as subjects attempt a double assimilation into a class and a culture.

Since their social position is so fragile and their elevation so recent, the nouveaux riches are particularly unsure how to regard themselves and others in class terms, many being arrivistes who are not sure if they've arrived. Some are especially worried about accusations of being "trailer trash" or (if Black) "ghetto." (Rather desperately, some Black women on *The Real Housewives of Atlanta* seize on the title "southern belle," ignoring the historical fact that their ancestors were more likely slaves than plantation owners.) As mentioned, TV figures frequently judge someone or something as simply "classy," a term which some would insist makes one déclassé. People are also judged to "have class" or be "a class act," a nomenclature that appears to nullify everyone inevitably occupying *some* class position due to unequal societal arrangements; instead, it makes "having class" in general an honorific conceivably open to all. Online discussions indicate that a central, and for some viewers delicious, tension is the gap between the subjects' self-conscious discussions about what constitutes "class" and their own vulgar behavior. While these figures lack accurate self-awareness, their relation to class is very self-conscious. Indeed, some have tried to cash in on the interest in class, as when LuAnn de Lesseps penned the etiquette book *Class with the Countess* (2009). That their wealth has not protected or elevated them from the same neediness that most people experience is perhaps what makes some sympathetic as well as cautionary examples. Viewers ponder if, for example, wealth and fame drain the genuine from personal relationships by commodifying them. When wealthy and when touched by RTV, people appear to no longer have genuine friends but instead employees or associates. Viewers find this Midas touch either sad or repugnant.

Upper class

The truly upper class is the rarest rank of all on RTV. Its members appear occasionally on British programming but in America, where producers and viewers don't appear to be sure what constitutes upper-class, old money is largely absent. At most, we see wealthy bourgeoisie and a few oligarchs: brash, self-made types who are easy to ridicule. Rarely does RTV offer a realistic view of even high-end corporate culture: instead we are given fake boardrooms and capitalism as a game (*The Apprentice*). In the US, there are occasional glimpses of socialites (*NYC Prep*, Bravo

2009; *The Simple Life*, Fox 2003–5, E! 2006–7) and the very wealthy appear as clients on high-end real estate, matchmaking, or concierge shows, as well as display shows like *Cribs* (MTV 2000–). But it is still predominantly self-made fortunes. We are more likely to see the upper class of a minor sort on British RTV as experts in cooking shows (*Two Fat Ladies*, BBC2 1996–9) or makeovers (*What Not to Wear*; *Changing Rooms*), as etiquette instructors (*Ladette to Lady*, ITV 2005–10) or socialites (*Made in Chelsea*). Rarely do we encounter titled aristocrats, just media/ image culture aspirants like almost everyone else on RTV. Class antagonism also occasionally erupts against the upper class, as when "Nasty Nick" (upper-class, southern, devious) lost to Craig (working-class, northern, honest) in the UK's *Big Brother* first season. Or when viewers were invited to scoff at the elite in *The Simple Life*, where in an almost Marxist cartoon the rich avoid labor and get the lower orders to do it for them (Hendershot 2009: 255).

Occasionally, being upper class is a hidden identity to create suspense as in *Undercover Princes* (BBC3 2009–; TLC 2012–) – although its subjects aren't as aristocratic as the producers make out and they confuse aristocratic title with being "royal." In America the confusion is considerable. Hence *The Kardashians'* Scott Disick claims he bought a "lordship" online to acquire the one thing America can't offer (aristocratic titles being forbidden by the constitution). How to recognize and treat aristocracy is an uncommon topic in American media but it became a talking point on *The Real Housewives of New York City* when one participant flaunted her Countess title and was quietly trumped by a later cast member who was entitled to call herself Princess. Some etiquette shows highlight upper-class behavior as a performance. *Ladette to Lady* supposedly trains lower-class women to be decorative hostesses and, though it clearly castigates lower-class behavior, it can also be seen as satirizing some quaint upper-class English habits. It is class teasing ultimately since, as in *Pygmalion/My Fair Lady*, the scheme is a profitable experiment that leads nowhere for its pupils. A variation involves the US mimicking of "royalty" in beauty pageants, which in one British series is framed as an American makeover of the inadequacies of British culture (*ASBO Teen to Beauty Queen*, C5 2006).[15]

Conclusion

Reality TV has encouraged some awareness of class and wealth hierarchies. How viewers respond to its portraits will depend upon their own situation and political beliefs, but class baiting, class envy, and wealth voyeurism currently generate solid ratings. Class is therefore not evaded but showcased and tried.

7

Politics

In most entertainment, media scholars agree, political effects are largely indirect, non-deterministic, and hegemonic. Certainly "manifest political content" is relatively low in RTV compared to news, documentary, or even some talk shows and drama (Corner 2010: 24). On RTV series there is generally no expository frame and no "propositional accounts" such as documentarians use to make explicit claims and arguments (Corner 2010: 25). Extra-diegetic narration or voiceovers are uncommon: which is not to say that there aren't less direct cues and framing of material. What is or isn't represented, and how what is represented is treated by producers or interpreted by viewers, these of course come out of and feed into a larger political context. Occasionally RTV programming has produced direct and demonstrable political effects – parliamentary debates, government regulations, bans, riots, resignations – which usually occur when a new series first appears or is about to appear.[1] But while across the globe RTV shows have provoked debates about issues that are essentially political, these have generally not been pursued far, examined deeply, or necessarily been acknowledged as political. Rather than there being a concerted or deliberate agenda on the producer's part, there is in media entertainment more typically a *confluence of individual aims – creative and commercial* – that intermingle on a sub-political level. These may create a predominant political effect, but as Graeme Turner has astutely observed, most media must be understood as "ideologically casual" and commercially serious (2010: 63). This is a crucial statement. Indeed, one can argue that the one (being casually ideological) follows from the other (commercial pressure) given that producers need to avoid seriously alienating viewers and losing ratings. Indeed, one of the most common observations made about reality TV is that it is depoliticized,[2] meaning it has no explicit political message or agenda, which is itself a political stance of sorts: in this case, a conservatism in favor of ratings and profit. An explicit political stance can be bad for business: not only might it upset and alienate a subset of the audience but, more importantly, political controversy can scare off advertisers. A certain amount of depoliticization is due also to the fact that television reaches large numbers of people but doesn't reach them collectively as a group.

None of this precludes viewers recognizing and analyzing the political dimensions of this or any other content, even if these are largely subterranean. Certainly media scholars are often attuned to political resonances and most agree that, not surprisingly, the dominant codes in this popular programming offer hegemonic support for the status quo. RTV's often superficial and truncated treatments tend to de-contextualize and so disable any critical inquiry into economic inequality, into the links between crime and poverty, into the agenda behind the relentless imperative for individuals to make something of themselves or blame themselves if they don't. Also largely unquestioned is the showcasing of the pleasures of consumer society and the rewarding of the competitive individualism that supports this system and, with it, mockery of those who don't succeed. On the other hand, we have also seen on some formats a more progressive attitude to gay identity, or race, or physical disabilities, more in line with the perspective of a desirable youthful demographic.

RTV likes to dazzle people with shortcuts and so instead of promoting or recording slow political reform, it traces the more dramatic trajectory of people who've become suddenly successful or rich. Or it features people who advocate a by-passing of political awareness and reliance on luck or divine inspiration. A good deal of RTV is about ordinary people attempting to make a sudden socio-economic advance, but ultimately this is only for the few and often with the aid of others (e.g., media companies). As indicated, another area where RTV perhaps mirrors larger social trends is its fundamental model of packaging and selling reality – this being a core mechanism also of modern politics whose *relations with the public* have increasingly shrunk to *public relations* (PR). RTV therefore reflects a political milieu of oblique rhetoric where truth or reality is regarded as something one can create and sell (Deery 2012). In addition, image, exhibitionism, and display of extreme positions are features both of RTV and of professional politics.

Media content is politically significant if we assume there is a progression from awareness, to knowledge, to understanding, to tolerance or liking, to political expression or engagement. This may indeed happen, but whether a viewer undergoes this process is, again, difficult to determine. Politicians – Presidents and Prime Ministers included – have occasionally used RTV as a platform to reach voters. In America, the highly patriotic and wholesome *Extreme Makeover: Home Edition* attracted two First Ladies and numerous state governors, while a rarely reticent former governor headlined her own *Sarah Palin's Alaska* (TLC 2010–11). In Britain, to take one example, British MP George Galloway appeared in *Celebrity Big Brother* (2006) and sparked a debate about whether this role debased politicians or was a savvy PR move. Galloway claimed he wanted to promote a political stance (opposition to the Iraq war) but complained that his remarks were often omitted (Ruddock 2010). Sometimes influence works in the other direction, as when Alan Sugar's time on the UK *Apprentice* brought him a political appointment as the British Government's Enterprise Tsar (Biressi 2011: 144), or when a top executive from *Big Brother* was hired by the Conservative Party to see if he could drum up votes for politicians too (Andrejevic 2010: 58). Anita Biressi (2011) also notes an instance of government sanction when *Benefit Busters* (a series designed to help the unemployed get work) had the blessing of the British government (p. 145).

Ordinary citizens have also attempted to make a political impact through RTV, as when Merlin Luck participated on the Australian *Big Brother* (2004) to advocate for refugees. His political comments were also largely edited out, but his final stunt of taping his mouth in his eviction interview revved up interest in the show even if it didn't have much political impact. The Brown family acknowledges that they went on *Sister Wives* to change attitudes and laws about polygamy, and it seems they succeeded to some extent.[3] Jamie Oliver has also had some success in affecting policies regarding school meals (Williams 2010). His agenda to effect political change is reflected in titles like *Jamie's Ministry of Food* (C4 2008) or *Jamie Oliver's Food Revolution* (ABC 2010–11), and he and other participants have met with senior politicians and given evidence to an Education Select Committee. The winner of *Election* (BBC 2008), a competition that tested different skills for political office, met with the British Prime Minister, while *El Candidato de la Gente* (Argentina 2002) viewers were invited to select a candidate for real-life legislative elections (Kraidy 2010: 36). But these direct interchanges are rare. The rest of this chapter will survey what scholars have identified as RTV's more latent political content, particularly its reflection or anticipation of forms of regulation and control such as neoliberal governmentality, surveillance, and the collective identity of nationalism.

Neoliberalism and governmentality

Essentially a laissez-faire form of capitalism, neoliberalism promotes privatization, deregulation, self-reliance, and (tacitly or explicitly) the withdrawal of public or social services. Its proponents advocate a global "free trade" with a weakening of labor organization.[4] The media industry increasingly functions within this paradigm and embraces its principles both in production practices and content. The appearance of neoliberal thinking on RTV, particularly in its makeover programming, was noted early on by several scholars (among them, Dovey 2000; Palmer 2003; Andrejevic 2004; Ouellette 2004; Sender 2006; McCarthy 2007; Couldry 2008; Ringrose and Walkerdine 2008) and was brought to prominence by Laurie Ouellette and James Hay (2008) whose impressive book-length study draws on Foucault to relate neoliberalism and governmentality. Governmentality describes a Foucauldian indirect governance or government-at-a-distance that relies on the citizen's self-scrutiny and self-regulation and an internalizing of normative discourses under the rubric of choice and freedom.[5] In other words, governmentality is a mechanism suited to a neoliberal society intent on reducing public funding and support.

Reality TV reaches into the real world and impacts real people, many of whom can serve as models (positive or negative) for those watching. Hence, scholars argue, this type of media can intentionally or unintentionally take on a civic role, replacing social programs with television programs that model proper citizenship. Usually RTV is conceived of as working independently of government but in tune with politicians' attempts both in the US and UK to "reinvent government" in a post-welfare society. In particular, commentators see evidence of neoliberal governmentality in makeover and advice shows that offer guides to self-management. For example, Ron Becker incisively argues that nanny/parenting shows reinforce the neoliberal faith in individual growth and responsibility and, ignoring state resources, put the burden on the isolated nuclear family to produce good citizens and a stable society. Here, as elsewhere, the TV experts provide temporary rather than structural help (Becker 2006). Tania Lewis (2014), among others, notes that much makeover programming has the effect of reducing citizenship and civic culture to questions of privatized consumer choice (p. 411). One agenda of neoliberalism is to depoliticize politics, as Mark Andrejevic (2010) notes, meaning it emphasizes individual decision making (and responsibility) within a market rather than a public sphere. But it could be that RTV's get-rich-quick formats, by short-circuiting a meritocratic path to success, are interfering with the official neoliberal script: certainly Kimberly Springer (2014) suggests this is true of Britain with its more entrenched class definitions and expectations that social advancement will be based on more than fame or luck.

Occasionally there are formal partnerships between RTV series and privately or publicly funded organizations intent on educating citizens or changing social attitudes. Laurie Ouellette (2014a) traces such cooperation in teenage pregnancy shows that provide online "study guides" and other forms of institutional outreach but neglect to mention government welfare programs. The much earlier *America's Most Wanted* (1988–), coproduced with the FBI's Public Affairs Office, could also be regarded as training the citizenry. Observers identify in some makeover programming what has become known as social entrepreneurship (e.g., Ouellette and Hay 2008; Biressi 2011; Deery 2012), a move that some critics read as insinuating that socialism is a spent force (e.g., Leggott and Hochscherf 2010: 54). Social entrepreneurship entails private individuals or organizations providing aid in place of government programs and as encouraged by governmental rhetoric such as Cameron's "Big Society."[6] Often this privatized giving functions as a Public Relations and brand-building exercise (Deery 2012).

Since earlier and very productive discussions of governmentality and neoliberalism, some RTV scholars have proposed modifications or further contextualizations. For instance, as a pragmatic matter, audience studies suggest that most viewers don't accept what producers cue or experts advise and so TV's social intervention may in fact be weak (e.g., Skeggs and Wood 2009, 2012; B. Weber 2009; Sender 2012). Indeed, a concern with a program's possible pedagogic effect may miss the pleasures of resisting advice or of viewers simply laughing at bad behavior, or bad productions. Moreover, audience studies reiterate that individual viewers can and do interpret modeled behavior differently depending on their class/race/gender or life experience. As for contextualization, media sociologist Nick Couldry (2011a) situates RTV's neoliberalism and governmentality within a broader attempt by the media to claim authority in accessing social reality. Urging citizens to improve or regulate the self is part of the media's larger aim to define and adjudicate social values. What are identified as neoliberal practices on reality TV (e.g., self-enterprise, consumerism, privatized aid) may also be understood within a fundamental and primary commercial framework, where it is important to observe the distinction between the media's ideological and economic motivations: the one is not divorced from the other but the latter is easier to substantiate, as when privatized aid functions as advertising.

Meanwhile, studies of the global market suggest that neoliberalism cannot be regarded as monolithic. While it encourages the easy movement of capital and thus facilitates TV production, it is not necessarily universally embraced as RTV content. In some Arab or Asian countries viewers and/or their governing bodies may contest or resist neoliberalism and so in such places RTV isn't always working to promote this version of modernity (Kraidy 2011). Or in a highly regulated state like Singapore, Tania Lewis (2014) suggests the (broadly) neoliberal shaping of behavior in RTV makeovers works in conjunction with government initiatives rather than as a substitute for them and appeals to civic and community values rather than individualism.

Surveillance

Surveillance and its impact on privacy and democratic rights is clearly a major contemporary concern. It is also RTV's basic mode of operation. Hence commentators have identified RTV as emblematic of a new sociopolitical order. Mark Andrejevic (2004) early on made a convincing argument that the nature of RTV helps acclimatize viewers to intimate and increasingly pervasive forms of surveillance, to the benefit of both governmental and commercial interests (see also Couldry 2004; Bignell 2005). Whether or not this is the producer's direct agenda, much RTV programming associates surveillance with positive values like individualism, self-expression, and authenticity, in addition to monetary rewards (Andrejevic 2004). Today, whether due to social media or revelations about government surveillance, privacy appears to be eroding or certainly under negotiation. Some RTV surveillance is surreptitious, but more commonly it is overt. Both participants and viewers know subjects are being watched, but typically the act of surveillance, the physical evidence of cameras and crew, doesn't appear on camera. So the surveillance is known but in this sense hidden. Less commonly, a format depends on completely hidden surveillance, going back to the early progenitor of *Candid Camera*, a Cold War hit that grew out of military recording technology. *Candid Camera*, it seems, worked in two ways: it laughed off anxieties about being surveilled and it laughed at those who conform (Clissold 2004; McCarthy 2004; Kavka 2012). This set-up, with less political resonance, continues today in comic formats like *Punk'd* or *Disaster Date* (MTV 2009–11). There are also occasional ad hoc hidden cameras within a show or peer sousveillance, as when docusoap participants tape and replay each other's phone calls.

Other series attempt to turn hostile and authoritarian surveillance into entertainment not by playing it for laughs and not to benefit those being watched. Often it is a business or property matter. For example, spying on employees becomes central in *Tabatha Takes Over* (Bravo 2008–) or *Restaurant Stakeout* (Food Network 2012), and surveillance is used to catch criminals, adulterers (*Cheaters*), or just unreliable businesses (*Tradesmen from Hell*, LifeStyle 2004). But entrapment formats can be seen as unfair and themselves predatory. The self-righteous and sanctimonious host on *Cheaters*, who poses as only there to extract justice rather than make a salacious TV show, is often challenged by those being filmed, and there are claims that the show's producers are cheating by paying actors to participate. More respectable is the secret filming of behavior in *What Would You Do?* that is presented as a sociological experiment – an original but less often heard rationale for *Big Brother*. When legal authorities are involved, as in *To Catch a Predator* (MSNBC 2004–7), this prompts questions such as: Is TV now an arm of the law? Is this programming making a positive social impact, or is it TV vigilantism using public exposure as a preemptive form of punishment? (One suspect committed suicide in order to avoid public exposure.) A seemingly more benign form of semi-hidden surveillance can be found on *Undercover Boss*, where the camera is visible but is falsely represented as surveilling someone else, someone who is disguising their power in this situation (the boss). Most workers come out looking good and show no apparent resentment of the trickery or the surveillance, nor of the economic disparities they reveal.

More often the surveillance on reality TV is voluntary and

overt, a combination that has a particular political interest. On a gamedoc that invokes and apparently defuses Orwell's nightmare, surveillance is thematized and nearly absolute (*Big Brother*). The act of surveillance is also foregrounded on *Room Raiders* (MTV 2004–), a series that light-heartedly examines the intimate contents of a potential date's bedroom: on *Room Raiders 2.0* contestants extend this surveillance to checking all kinds of personal media devices, thus exemplifying the social data mining in today's personal relationships. Subjects clearly undergo involuntary surveillance on a series like *Cops* which places viewers on the side of the police (riding along with them); though one study found that at least Black viewers resisted this positioning because they judged the content racist (McNair 2010). Other shows that purport to display illegal acts, such as *Moonshiners*, put viewers in an empathetic relationship with the perpetrators (who must volunteer to be surveilled), although the law enforcers (who also agree to be filmed) are often quite sympathetically drawn as well.[7] Also skirting the law is *Overhaulin'* (TLC 2004–9) where producers take someone's car to renovate it but the owner is made to think it is stolen or impounded, with some participants even impersonating police officers. Pseudo surveillance is an aesthetic element on *Mob Wives* (VH1 2011–) where graphics and camerawork mimic police surveillance tape. Although, ironically, this show also involved a real but hidden surveillance when one ex-husband pretended to reconcile with his former wife only to tape her father's conversations for the police (he's now in a witness protection program). By the time this was broadcast many viewers would have known about this betrayal and watched the wife being taken in, adding another layer of recording with high stakes in real life that even the RTV producers didn't know about.

Some surveillance can be regarded as therapeutic and a useful motivator; for example, being watched by millions may put positive pressure on someone to change behavior (e.g., weight loss) (Sender 2012). Certainly, many RTV denizens compete in order to be watched and their eventual prizes or better outcomes become, as Mark Andrejevic observed, "an advertisement for the benefits of submissions to comprehensive surveillance" (2004: 2). The overt and exaggerated nature of much RTV surveillance could be read as reassuring, as with *Candid Camera* in its Cold War context. When reality shows use surveillance in hyperbolic and artificial environments they could distract from, or reduce the fear of, the more insidious surveillance in everyday life, whether on computer or CCTV screens. Jean Baudrillard remarked once that Disneyland's artificiality makes the rest of America seem more real but hides the fact that it isn't (1983: 25). He revisited this analogy when commenting on the French series *Loft Story* (M6 2001–2) to conclude that the contrived nature of this RTV show hides that our own lives are also artificial (Baudrillard 2001). So to dismiss reality TV as simply fake may protect some people's sense of the reality of their own experience.

Globalism

RTV formats are still predominantly developed in Northern Europe and America, but they provide a good example of *glocalization*, of products that have cultural flexibility but local appeal.[8] The same economics attract producers worldwide and many RTV formats are sufficiently adaptable to attract high ratings in diverse cultures, these adaptations reminding us that television is still often geared to national audiences. The international format trade has undergone great growth in the last two decades. Importing already successful formats not only provides a reassuring track record for producers and advertisers but also fulfills quotas for domestic production when these are in place. When a format is franchised the industrial knowledge on offer may include the program "bible" (production instructions), on-site consultants, computer software, graphics, sound, ratings data, promotional material, and scripts (Moran 2014). Large players in international format development are Endemol (Holland), FremantleMedia (UK), and the BBC. As Marwan Kraidy's (2010) important study of the Middle East reveals, in some parts of the world there is a transnational production in which programs are filmed in one country, broadcast from another, and watched in several others.

While this study has focused on programming in America and Britain where the same formats are easily traded back and forth, across the world there are different relations between government, viewers, and the media arising from different socio-economic and political arrangements. This inevitably affects content. Generally speaking, producers want to know how best to attract a new audience by being provocative if necessary but without offending too many people or coming under official censure. Scholars are interested in how dramatic structures and participant behavior change when a program is imported and what this might reveal about a culture: for example, to what extent formats are confrontational or cooperative, or if they promote individualism or group identity. Studies today have become wider in scope to include RTV programming in Asia, Africa, the Middle East, Latin America, and Australia.[9] For example, scholars report that Arab and Chinese programming is more didactic and less inclined to debase and humiliate subjects than Western RTV formats.[10] Asian formats appear more community oriented, with less focus on individual competition and financial gain and more incorporation of government concerns (Lewis 2011, 2014; Yang 2014). On Asian shows it seems there is more cultural reserve about exposing oneself and one's lifestyle (Lewis 2011: 84). Chinese RTV tends to be patriotic and liable to government censorship, with official objections to too much individual competition, gambling, sex, or nudity (Luo 2010: 176). But as Chinese society and media are becoming somewhat less regulated and commercial forces compete with government authority, RTV formats now appear to be playing roles similar to those in Western countries, as when makeover and advice shows help viewers navigate new consumer opportunities (Lewis 2014) or when meritocratic competitions possibly alleviate anxieties about growing structural inequalities (Sun and Zhao 2009, quoted in Yang 2014).

Controversies and scandals when they serve marketing purposes can be quite beneficial for producers. They also open up spaces for public discussion of topics that are otherwise taboo. When imported values or cultural memes upset the indigenous status quo, citizens' reactions reveal schisms and tensions within the host country: between rulers and citizens, between the religious and the secular, and between generations. RTV often exhibits unlicensed behavior and so sparks debates about acceptable limits and, ultimately, matters of authority. Common debates center on differences in social mores (gender, race) or political organization (democratic or more autocratic): indeed controversies often illustrate how religious, social, and political structures are interrelated (e.g., gender regulation is both political and religious). RTV is sometimes objected to as importing "Western values" such as capitalist competition, individualism, secularism, sexual promiscuity, with especially heated rhetoric opposing East and West in Middle Eastern contexts. A Pan-Arab *Big Brother* was quickly cancelled in 2004 after a public outcry and street protests, while one Imam in Mecca dubbed *Star Academy* a "weapon of mass destruction" and others have used language like "moral terrorism" (Kraidy 2010: 100, 101). RTV has given rise to debates in strict regimes where such public airing of ideas is not encouraged. Marwan Kraidy notes that "Like a chemical developer bringing latent patterns into crisp view, contention over reality TV brings simmering social and political tensions to the surface of public life" (2010: 193). Not surprisingly, it is often a dispute between old-guard, traditional authorities and more liberal, youthful viewers. For example, gender roles are a strong indicator of differences between and within societies and become the issue through which people discuss privacy, individual rights, and religious orthodoxy. A fatwa issued in Saudi Arabia forbade anyone from watching or participating in their version of *Star Academy* particularly because of what is referred to as "the free mixing of the sexes." Among other things, the show was decried for exploiting young women's bodies for commercial gain (Kraidy 2010: 103). And while the rhetoric may be extreme, such protests highlight questions that perhaps should be more often heard in the West, such as whether women's appearances on RTV are indeed emancipatory or demeaning.

Some Middle Eastern broadcasters appear torn between seizing the commercial opportunities of RTV programming and upholding traditional values regarding religion and patriarchy (Kraidy 2010). Satellite technology means that states have less control over what their citizens watch and RTV importation illustrates how global capitalism can trump state control or national identity. It even precipitates questions about political ontology: for example, Kraidy (2010) notes that, prior to the arrival of RTV, state-controlled media production in several Middle Eastern countries was generally known to be manipulated and not a faithful representation of the real lives of its populace. By prompting questions about what is reality and who defines it, RTV has sparked debates about the legitimacy of those in political authority who claim the right to do so. This obviously is a contentious issue, as whoever claims to represent reality also claims to determine what is normal and desirable. Authenticity in these instances is a political idea and is judged by political or moral authorities. This is different from judgments about whether a TV participant is being themselves or how much producers manipulate and stage. Whatever the issue, the sparking of political debate is ultimately a by-product of the commercial push to attract viewers, with novel or outlandish behavior if necessary.

Nationalism

National boundaries may have less force in today's global economy but they are still commercially useful in cultural production. Despite capital flowing internationally, the passions of patriotism and nationhood can be tapped locally: for example, to generate pride in a sentimental community in the context of war (*Extreme Makeover: Home Edition*) or other international rivalries (*Arabs Got Talent; Big Brother Africa*). Instead of appearing as state propaganda, nationalism in these instances is portrayed as a consumer demand and bottom-up impetus (Volcic and Andrejevic 2011: 116). Producers can exploit tensions and affiliations within one nation (like India) or between nations (Middle Eastern states) to encourage viewer engagement. In various versions of *Idol* around the world, and inspired more by regional pride than by an objective judging of singing ability, viewers have mobilized to vote collectively. Enthusiastic viewers of *Indian Idol* (SET 2004) have set up telephone voting booths, distributed pre-paid mobile phone cards, hired people to vote, and funded marketing campaigns, all to promote a regional favorite (Punathambekar 2011). In 2007, its *Idol* fan clubs morphed into political party offices and mobilized to effect political change (Punathambekar 2011: 141). Other countries have instead attempted to use RTV to perform international diplomacy: for example, to improve the image of the US abroad, some former high-ranking US government officials funded an RTV show for broadcast in the Middle East called *On the Road in America* (2007) featuring Middle Eastern students and a mostly positive impression (McMurria 2009: 195–6). *Terrorism in the Grip of Justice* (2005), an Iraqi program funded by the US-led Coalition Provisional Authority with footage provided by the Interior Ministry, followed forces pursuing and interrogating suspects and suggested that insurgents were essentially hired guns, not patriots (McMurria 2009: 195).

Other domestic RTV programming may be performing on a less conscious level as a political compensation for international failures or frustrations, simply because producers are tapping into a common zeitgeist in order to engage with viewers who occupy a particular political landscape. I have argued that in the post 9/11 *Extreme Makeover: Home Edition* the successful completion of cooperative tasks could represent a desire to compensate for failure to deliver on promised makeovers – or "nation building" – in a larger geopolitical context (Deery 2012). This long-running series often honored individuals who served in Iraq or Afghanistan with sentimental narratives promoting national pride and unquestioning support for the war. Against a campaign that never seemed to end, each episode offered definite results and clear victories. Weak structures and hidden dangers were objectively identified and swiftly replaced or fortified. From the other side, the Iraqi RTV series *Labor and Materials* (2004) provided families who lost homes and possessions due to American bombing with home makeovers. On both sides, popular television became a war strategy, as is cogently argued by James Hay (2011).

Militarism is, of course, a major component of nationalism: after all, nations are defined by their ability to organize for war

and citizens by their willingness to fight. Whereas the media generally ignore the fundamentally militaristic base of the American or
British economies, sentimental references to military life do appear
on RTV, typically reinforcing the connection to nation, family,
home, sacrifice, and duty. In the US, *Extreme Makeover: Home
Edition* was a particularly sentimental portrait and on British
television there are several very positive depictions of military or
police operations that showcase impressive equipment – especially
surveillance devices – and professional behavior. In many instances
the theme is the rescue or protection of ordinary civilians by dedicated and caring people in uniform: from an unending stream of
"cops" shows (including helicopter units) to programs featuring the Royal Air Force. Also in recent years militarism figures
prominently but metaphorically when "war" is used to describe
competition formats. This could be seen as domesticating a foreign
trauma and compensating for its failures – not unlike the "Rambo
effect" of compensating for the quagmire of Vietnam by projecting
success and glory on screen. Then there are economic fears. Early
on there were militaristic puns like the British *Homefront* (BBC
1996–2000) and *Ground Force* (BBC 1997–2005), but especially
since 2008 – and its economic insecurity – there has been a slew of
titles in the US such as *Parking Wars* (A&E 2008), *Storage Wars*
(A&E 2010–), *Property Wars* (Discovery 2012–), and *Shipping
Wars* (A&E 2012). Competition has become combat, as in *Top
Chef Duels* (Bravo 2014) and the preposterously named *Cupcake
Wars* (Food Network 2010–) whose mock heroic host enthuses:
"The battle for cupcake domination will be legendary!" This kind
of remark could be seen as trivializing war, during a time when the
longest campaign in US history drags on.

Some series feature actual military exercises and service members
who compete, judge, or train others, often due to official arrangements and alliances; from *Boot Camp* (Fox 2001), made with
the cooperation of the US marine corps, to *Homeland Security
USA* (ABC 2004–9) and *Commando VIP* (Five 2005). In Israel,
one *Idol* series took place in a military base and featured judges
wearing army uniforms (Neiger 2012). *Married to the Army:
Alaska* (OWN 2012) and *Surprise Homecoming* (TLC 2011)

take a more domestic and feminine approach to project a positive view of American military families, reflecting a White House initiative (Michelle Obama's "Joining Forces"). The gamedoc *Stars Earn Stripes* (NBC 2012) – produced by former British soldier and *Survivor* creator Mark Burnett – was hosted by retired NATO Supreme Allied Commander Wesley Clark and followed a group of celebrities competing (for charity) in various challenges based on actual US military training exercises. Eight Nobel Peace Laureates demanded the program be cancelled for glorifying war and making its horrors into entertainment.

Democratization

Finally, some (more often journalists than scholars) argue that RTV is democratic or is a democratizing force, usually because it involves ordinary people and/or because it encourages voting. Of course, RTV's possible political significance will depend upon each society's extant political context; for example, how much ordinary people already participate in the political process. If "democratic" is being used in the broadest sense of participation and involvement of "the people," then there are some grounds for its application here. But to claim that reality programming increases or enhances the democratic structure of a society is, for most scholars, quite a stretch: after all, the involvement of ordinary people doesn't represent a significant difference in power relations even within the media industry. Employing ordinary people is intended to attract viewers and cut production costs, not give voice to the powerless. However, having said that, in countries where there is no general franchise viewers being allowed to vote can be seen as influencing or commenting on national politics. Certainly nervous Chinese authorities have allowed and then cancelled RTV voting (Yang 2014) and a year after the state-run newspaper *Beijing Today* ran the headline: "Is *Super Girl* a Force for Democracy?" (2005), the government banned this talent competition outright. Kraidy (2010) argues that in the Middle East RTV can be seen as having a democratizing effect if democracy is defined as "popular contention, deliberation, and performance," but involving informal deliberations rather than formal elections (p. 199).

In Western democracies, voting in response to a reality show is perhaps better characterized as "demotic," a term Graeme Turner (2010) employs to refer to an increased visibility of ordinary people without an increase in their power. In fact, one could argue that RTV most typically functions as a political distraction or compensation. It short circuits political activity due to a *false equivalence*, if the empowerment a viewer feels by voting for their favorite singer distracts them from their lack of engagement in the larger political sphere. In established democracies, commentators note with concern that sometimes more votes are cast in a talent show than in a national election.[11] Viewer voting can therefore be seen as symptomatic of the public's distrust of elite politicians or even the political process. Francois Jost suggests that RTV programs remedy the defects attributed to politicians by showing ordinary, sincere, and powerless people who are subject to the viewer's vote (2011: 42). They give voice to the ordinary person away from smooth, professional, political rhetoric. I would add that to the extent that RTV is also stage-managed, its voting opportunities could suggest that national politics, too, is an image-driven game for the profit of the few designed to exploit and entertain the many. Such cynicism, as Corner (2010) points out, might have the effect of disengaging viewers from politics and may invite them to judge political performances with the same amused detachment they adopt when watching reality TV (p. 37).

Conclusion

Not surprisingly, RTV producers aren't particularly interested in politics. But if we accept that every social representation is ultimately political and its political significance is available for analysis, then examining the politics of reality TV is another legitimate approach to understanding its significance. RTV has sometimes had a direct impact on politics (parliamentary debates) and its content can be seen as mimicking (voting) or enacting political ideas and techniques (governmentality, surveillance). Its discourse and drama are now integrated into many cultures around the world, none more so than in America and Britain. Eyes may roll, but they also watch – and knowing what they are watching will enrich any observer's understanding of the contemporary scene.

Notes

I Introduction: Definitions, History, Critiques

1 For example, President Obama said of the Republican candidate debates in 2012 that he was going to "wait until everybody's voted off the island."

2 In the UK, RTV programs appear on Channel 4 (C4), E4, More 4, Dave, Sky 3, Living 2, Discovery Real Time, Watch, Home, and Really and in the US, Bravo, TLC, E!, History, HGTV, A&E, MTV, WE, VH1, Style and several others.

3 That RTV is fundamentally about a way of making television is also underlined by Andrejevic (2014).

4 For more on international format trading, see essays by Raphael (2004), Magder (2009), and McMurria (2009); also Kraidy (2010) and Moran (2014).

5 By para-journalistic I mean those who are not employed by mainstream newspapers or broadcasters but who may have some readership and standing in online forums.

6 Specifically, I grew up in Northern Ireland watching mostly British media and have lived in America for the last 20 years, visiting the UK every year.

7 *Unsolved Mysteries* reappeared on CBS (1997–9) and Lifetime (2001–2, 2010–).

8 Although *Crimewatch* was an early British law-and-order format (BBC 1984).

9 There are some precedents in the radio series *Nightwatch* (1951–5), which recorded the daily activities of police officers in Culver City, California.

10 In 1978, *Living in the Past* recreated life in an Iron Age English village.

11 The first version of *Survivor*, called *Expedition Robinson*, appeared in 1997 in Sweden. A similar program called *Castaways* (BBC 2000) was more documentary than gamedoc. The Dutch series *Nummer 28* (1991) also put

strangers together for an extended period and included "confessionals" recorded by cast members.

12 A tent pole is a successful show that holds audience interest for less-known shows scheduled beside it.

13 Fox Reality (US, 2005–10), Global Reality Channel (Canada, 2010–), and Zone Reality (UK, 2002–).

14 RTV has also inspired dramas and novels, such as Shields, G. (2006) *The Actual Real Reality of Jennifer James: A Reality TV Novel.* HarperTeen, New York.

15 Good overviews of RTV scholarship can be found in introductory chapters by, for example, Holmes and Jermyn (2004), Kavka (2012), and Ouellette (2014b).

2 Reality Status

1 Wendy Merrill in David (2010: 142).

2 Thanks to my student Margaret O'Connor for using RTV as a proper noun.

3 Mark Burnett refers to shows like his *Survivor* as "dramality." Biressi and Nunn (2005) use the term "non-fiction programming."

4 Biosphere 2 is a large greenhouse structure located in Arizona that is used to study ecological interdependence. In 1991, one "mission" required eight researchers to remain locked inside for two years.

5 Of course, actors reciting lines on stage is actual in the limited sense that audio-visual effects are really occurring, but they are portraying fictional events and so in that sense the experiences they portray are not actually happening to them.

6 For a brilliant and lively examination of authenticity and commercialization, though not specifically regarding reality television, see Banet-Weiser (2012).

7 Of course, it may not be possible to agree on what constitutes ordinary people (e.g., Hill 2007: 179).

8 This language comes from the *Home Edition* release form. Available from: http://a.abc.com/media/primetime/xtremehome/apply/2008_APPLICATION.pdf

9 For more details on this side of production, see the pioneering work of Vicki Mayer (2011a).

10 A less obviously scripted but also celebrity-driven early comdoc was *The Osbournes* (MTV 2002–5).

11 Erving Goffman's mid-century work on everyday performances has been particularly useful for RTV scholars.

12 Available from: http://www.bravotv.com/the-real-housewives-of-beverly-hills/season-1/blogs/bh-producers/show-some-love?page=0,5

13 The poignancy of the combined immediacy and pastness of CCTV crime footage is impressively demonstrated by Jermyn (2004).

14 Bravo's *The Real Housewives of Beverly Hills* executive producer Dave Rupel. Available from: http://www.bravotv.com/the-real-housewives-of-beverly-hills/season-1/blogs/bh-producers/go-behind-the-scenes-in-beverly-hil?page=0,1

15 For a more detailed, philosophical study of affect and embodiment in RTV, see Kavka (2014b).

16 2 Charged in Reality TV Staged Robbery. CBS Pittsburgh News, August 6, 2012. Available from: http://pittsburgh.cbslocal.com/2012/08/06/2-charged-in-reality-tv-staged-robbery/

17 For a comparison of RTV and documentary, see, e.g., Corner (2002), Biressi and Nunn (2005), and Palmer (2011).

18 See Hardy (1966: 147).

19 The Only Way Is Essex: A Masterclass. Edinburgh International Television Festival. 2011. Available from: http://www.youtube.com/watch?v=S-Ttaac6wdc&feature=related

3 Social Television: Reality TV and New Media

1 A decade ago ABC offered "enhanced TV" where viewers were invited to play along with a quiz show or answer questions synched to other broadcasts (Deery 2003: 178–9).

2 Coactive is when two or more devices are used at the same time.

3 It is thought that some viral videos or photos related to RTV series are emailed by PR agencies (Bignell 2005: 161).

4 *Honey Boo Boo* producers experimented with olfactory interactivity when they provided a watch-and-sniff card in *People Magazine*, July 17, 2013.

5 Producers discuss the making of TOWIE in a Masterclass at the 2011 Edinburgh International Television Festival. Available from: http://www.youtube.com/watch?v=S-Ttaac6wdc.

6 For example, the *Watch What Happens* Official Rules state that anyone who submits a comment agrees to grant NBC a license to use it as they see fit. Available from: http://www.bravotv.com/watch-what-happens-live/official-rules.

4 Advertising and Commercialization

1 A series like *Survivor* employs large numbers of people in exotic locations with considerable logistic, insurance, and security costs.

2 One minor success was when carpenters picketed the set of *The Real World* in Philadelphia (2004) and in a secret agreement got the producers to use some union labor (Collins 2008: 87–8). For other minor union victories, see Andrew Ross (2014).

3 Hendershot (2009) underlines how much RTV participation is essentially cheap labor.

4 For more details on placement frequency and business arrangements, see Magder (2009).
5 Public broadcasters like the BBC cannot place any products, unless in pro-gramming acquired elsewhere. The BBC is funded not by advertising but by annual user license fees at rates set by the government.
6 For earlier "pre-welfare" and sponsored charitable shows, see Watts (2009).
7 I explore the links between corporate sponsored makeovers and the rise of Public Relations in some detail in *Consuming Reality* (Deery 2012).
8 The Delivery Agent website enables viewers to purchase products they see on a TV show: more at deliveryagent.com.
9 For example, *Survivor* props were sold on e-bay, the proceeds going to an AIDS charity.
10 On *Watch What Happens Live*, aired April 22, 2012.
11 For an excellent brief overview of consumption, see Aldridge (2003).
12 I write in more detail about these shopping rituals in Deery (2012).

5 Gender and Race

1 My considering gender, race, and class separately is not to suggest that these are anything other than interdependent identities or that an intersectional approach is not optimum for many forms of in-depth study.
2 Judith Butler's (1990) work on gender as an enactment or performance has been highly influential, as has work by Anthony Giddens (1991) and Nikolas Rose (1996) on capitalist demands for self-enterprise and self-formation in a postindustrial society lacking traditional institutional guidelines.
3 For the enterprising self and reflexive consumer-based identity on RTV, see, e.g., Bonner (2003), Ouellette (2004), Palmer (2004), B. Weber (2009), Deery (2012), and Sender (2012).
4 In the US, Lifetime, TLC, and OWN broadcast predominately feminine pro-gramming, while History, Discovery, and National Geographic target men. Bravo appeals to a feminine and gay demographic.
5 One study found that more women watched lifestyle and gamedoc program-ming by at least a 2:1 margin in Britain and Sweden (Hill 2007: 66–7).
6 For a more detailed discussion of how this kind of intimate labor is exploited, see Andrejevic (2004, 2011).
7 It was a novelty when the second British *Wife Swap* series swapped husbands (Piper 2004: 275).
8 Scholarly analyses of cosmetic surgery examine gender implications, identity formation, and ties to neoliberalism; for example, Deery (2004b, 2006, 2012); Fraser (2007); Gailey (2007); Tait (2007); M. Jones (2008); B. Weber (2009).
9 For studies that find correlations between viewing makeover television and

having a positive attitude toward cosmetic surgery, see, e.g., Nabi (2009); Markey and Markey (2010).

10 Occasionally RTV features the grotesque results of surgery gone bad (e.g., the elderly Elsa in *The Real Housewives of Miami*).

11 See, for instance, Bessenoff (2006) and Tiggemann (2005).

12 Occasionally, a series will counter with affirmations about the beauty of larger bodies, as in *How to Look Good Naked* (C4 2006–10; Lifetime 2008) or *Mo'Nique's FAT Chance* (Oxygen 2005–7). But even in such series, less fat tends to be preferred over more fat; see B. Weber (2014: 374).

13 I have written more on RTV and surgery in Deery (2012).

14 For an early overview of gays on RTV, see Pullen (2004) and later Gamson (2014). See also Clarkson (2005); Miller (2006); Sender (2006); DiMattia (2007); Kavka (2008); Lewis (2008).

15 For a recent overview of racial representations on RTV, see Squires (2014).

16 In a 2012 lawsuit two African American males accused ABC of discriminating against them when casting for *The Bachelor*.

17 For an assessment of responses to *Black. White.* and other RTV shows featuring race, see Bell-Jordan (2008).

18 Drew (2011) argues that this series is pretending to be postracial but actually reinforces racial stereotypes.

19 Recent demographics in the USA are: 72% White, 16% Latino, 12.6% African, and 5% Asian (US 2010 Census). In the UK (2011): 86% White, 7% Asian, and 3% Black African or Caribbean (Office for National Statistics).

20 Interesting early examples of mixed race sitcoms were *Love Thy Neighbour* (ITV 1972–6) and the superior, educated African figure on *Rising Damp* (ITV 1974–8).

21 Goody herself was of mixed race (White and Black West Indian) and criticized for her facial features.

22 For more on "guido" as a chosen ethnicity, see Klein (2014). Interestingly, a trip to Italy confirmed the cast's distance from Italian culture.

6 Class

1 For accessible overviews of class, see Skeggs (2004), Devine et al. (2005), Bennett et al. (2009), Kendall (2011), and Biressi and Nunn (2013).

2 Perhaps the only organizations comfortable using "class" distinctions today are large commercial entities like airlines and hotel chains that base designations on the temporary ability to pay.

3 Tebbit was Thatcher's employment secretary.

4 For a consideration of class vs. status, see Crompton (2008).

5 For an account of how style and status have sometimes superseded class, see Ewen (1988) and Pakulski and Waters (1996).

6 In *Tower Block of Commons* (C4 2010) four Members of Parliament from

different parties spent time living in a variety of deprived housing estates around Britain.

7 For a detailed analysis of the Goody–Shetty exchange, see Tolson (2011).

8 For more on White studies, see, for example, Wray (2006) and Wray and Newitz (1996).

9 On macho programming, see Poniewozik (2008); also Kendall (2011) and Palmer (2014).

10 Nunn and Biressi (2014) argue for a less cynical reading of this series' sentimental narrative.

11 Ringrose and Walkerdine (2008: 238) designate the hosts as upper-class and Palmer (2004) and Kavka (2012) describe them as upper-middle.

12 Among others, Bonner (2003); Palmer (2003, 2004, 2011); Skeggs (2004); Skeggs and Wood (2009); McRobbie (2004).

13 One exception is the working-class expert (a real cleaner) on *How Clean is Your House?* (C4 2003–9).

14 For more on the Kardashians' ostentatious display and neoliberal family values, see Pramaggiore and Negra (2014).

15 An ASBO is an "anti-social behavior order" used to designate someone considered delinquent. It is a legal sentence passed by a judge that restricts people's movements or behavior.

7 Politics

1 For more on controversies and public outcry around the world, see Mathijs and Jones (2004), Biltereyst (2004), Kraidy (2010), and Kraidy and Sender (2011). For riots over racist comments in India, see Punathambekar (2011: 141).

2 Those who note depoliticization on RTV are too numerous to mention.

3 In December 2013 the Browns' lawsuit brought a change to Utah law regarding polygamy and allowed their family's co-habitation.

4 For a critical overview of neoliberalism, see Harvey (2007).

5 Governmentality is a theme across much of Foucault's writing but is clearly outlined in *Discipline and Punish* (1977 [1975]) and *The Foucault Effect: Studies in Governmentality* (Burchell et al. 1991).

6 As Nunn and Biressi (2014) document, the British government explicitly recognized the role of RTV in modeling privatized aid and expressed a desire to work with the media in promoting this agenda.

7 Police authorities claim *Moonshiners* shows only dramatizations not actual illegal acts.

8 Some shows sell their international flavor (*The Amazing Race*, CBS 2003–; *House Hunters International*, HGTV 1999–), but most adapt for the local culture.

9 For other global perspectives, see collections edited by Mathjis and Jones

(2004), Baruh and Park (2010), Kraidy and Sender (2011), as well as several articles in the journal *TV & New Media*.

10 Even Australian TV is judged by Tania Lewis to be less aggressive and humiliating than American or British formats. For other adaptations around the world, see also McMurria (2009).

11 The Conservative Party appointed a top executive from *Big Brother*'s production company to see if he could get people to vote for politicians as eagerly as they vote for RTV competitors (Andrejevic 2010: 58).

References

Adams, J. (1931) *The Epic of America*. Little, Brown, Boston, MA.

Aldridge, A. (2003) *Consumption*. Polity, Cambridge.

Andrejevic, M. (2004) *Reality TV: The Work of Being Watched*. Rowan & Littlefield, Lanham, MD.

Andrejevic, M. (2008) Watching television without pity: The productivity of online fans. *Television & New Media*, 9(1): 24–46.

Andrejevic, M. (2010) Reality TV is not democratic – it's psychotic. In: Baruh, L. and Park, J. (eds.) *Reel Politics: Reality Television as a Platform for Political Discourse*. Cambridge Scholars Publishing, Newcastle upon Tyne: 58–71.

Andrejevic, M. (2011) Real-izing exploitation. In: Kraidy, M. and Sender, K. (eds.) *The Politics of Reality Television: Global Perspectives*. Routledge, New York: 18–30.

Andrejevic, M. (2014) When everyone has their own reality show. In: Ouellette, L. (ed.) *A Companion to Reality Television*. Wiley Blackwell, Chichester: 40–56.

Andrejevic, M. and Colby, D. (2006) Racism and reality TV: The case of MTV's Road Rules. In: Escoffery, D. (ed.) *How Real is Reality TV? Essays on Representation and Truth*. McFarland, Jefferson, NC: 195–211.

Banet-Weiser, S. (2012) *Authentic: the Politics of Ambivalence in a Brand Culture*. New York University, New York.

Banet-Weiser, S. and Portwood-Stacer, L. (2006) "I just want to be me again!": Beauty pageants, reality television and post-feminism. *Feminist Theory*, 7(2): 255–72.

Baruh, L. and Park, J. (eds.) (2010) *Reel Politics: Reality Television as a Platform for Political Discourse*. Cambridge Scholars Publishing, Newcastle upon Tyne.

Battaglio, S. (2002) Big "Idol" winner: Fox. *Daily News*, September 6.

Baudrillard, J. (1983) *Simulations* (trans. P. Foss, P. Patton and P. Beitchman). Semiotext(e), New York.

References

Baudrillard, J. (1988 [1987]) *The Ecstasy of Communication* (trans. B. Schutze and C. Schutze). Semiotext(e), New York.

Baudrillard, J. (1993 [1990]) Operational whitewash. *The Transparency of Evil* (trans. J. Baddeley): 49–56. Verso, London.

Baudrillard, J. (1998 [1970]) *The Consumer Society* (trans. C. Turner). Sage, London.

Baudrillard, J. (2001) Dust breeding (trans F. Debrix). Available from: http//www.ctheory.net/text_file.asp?pick= 293.html.

Becker, R. (2006) "Help is on the way!": Supernanny, Nanny 911, and the neo-liberal politics of the family. In: Heller, D. (ed.) *The Great American Makeover: Television, History, Nation*. Palgrave Macmillan, New York: 175–91.

Bell-Jordan, K. (2008) *Black.White.* and a *Survivor* of *The Real World*: Constructions of race on reality TV. *Critical Studies in Media Communication*, 25(4): 353–72.

Bennett, T., Savage, M., Silva, E., Warde, A., Gayo-Cal, M. and Wright, D. (2009) *Culture, Class, Distinction*. Routledge, London.

Benza, J. (2005) *So You Wannabe on Reality TV?* Allworth Press, New York.

Berlant, L. (2011) *Cruel Optimism*. Duke University Press, Durham, NC.

Bessenoff, G. (2006) Can the media affect us? Social comparison, self-discrepancy, and the thin ideal. *Psychology of Women Quarterly*, 30: 239–51.

Bignell, J. (2005) *Big Brother: Reality TV in the Twenty-First Century*. Palgrave Macmillan, New York.

Bignell, J. (2014) Realism and reality formats. In: Ouellette, L. (ed.) *A Companion to Reality Television*. Wiley Blackwell, Chichester: 97–115.

Biltereyst, D. (2004) Reality TV, troublesome pictures and panics: Reappraising the public controversy around reality TV in Europe. In: Holmes, S. and Jermyn, D. (eds.) *Understanding Reality Television*. Routledge, New York: 91–110.

Biressi, A. (2011) The virtuous circle: Social entrepreneurship and welfare programming in the UK. In: Wood, H. and Skeggs, B. (eds.) *Reality Television and Class*. Palgrave Macmillan, New York: 144–55.

Biressi, A. and Nunn, H. (2005) *Reality TV: Realism and Revelation*. Wallflower, London.

Biressi, A. and Nunn, H. (2013) *Class and Contemporary British Culture*. Palgrave Macmillan, New York.

Black, J. (2002) *The Reality Effect*. Routledge, New York.

Bonner, F. (2003) *Ordinary Television: Analyzing Popular TV*. Sage, London.

Boorstin, D. (1992 [1961]) *The Image: A Guide to Pseudo-Events in America*. Vintage Books, New York.

Bordo, S. (1993) *Unbearable Weight: Feminism, Western Culture, and the Body*. University of California Press, Berkeley, CA.

Bratich, J. (2007) Programming reality: Control societies, new subjects and the powers of transformation. In: Heller, D. (ed.) *Makeover Television: Realities Remodelled*. I.B. Tauris, New York: 6–22.

References

Bratich, J. (2011) Affective convergence in reality television: a case study in divergence culture. In Kackman, M., Binfield, M., Payne, M.T., Perlman, A. and Sebok, B. (eds.) *Flow TV: Television in the Age of Media Convergence.* Routledge, New York: 55–74.

Burchell, G., Gordon, C. and Miller, P. (eds.) (1991) *The Foucault Effect: Studies in Governmentality.* University of Chicago, Chicago, IL.

Bussewitz, C. (2011) The altered realities of reality TV. *The Press Democrat*, 31 December.

Butler, J. (1990) *Gender Trouble: Feminism and the Subversion of Identity.* Routledge, New York.

Caudle, M. (2011) *The Reality of Reality TV: Reality Show Business Plans.* On the Lot Productions, New Orleans, LA.

Clarkson, J. (2005) Contesting masculinities makeover: Queer Eye, consumer masculinity and "straight acting" gays. *Journal of Communication Inquiry*, 29(3): 235–55.

Clissold, B. (2004) Candid Camera and the origins of reality TV: Contextualizing a historical precedent. In: Holmes, S. and Jermyn, D. (eds.) *Understanding Reality Television.* Routledge, New York: 33–53.

Collins, S. (2008) Making the most out of 15 minutes: Reality TV's dispensable celebrity. *Television & New Media*, 9(2): 87–110.

Corner, J. (2002) Performing the real: Documentary diversions. *Television & New Media*, 3(3): 255–69.

Corner, J. (2009) Performing the real: Documentary diversions (with afterword). In: Murray, S. and Ouellette, L. (eds.) *Reality TV: Remaking Television Culture*, 2nd edn. New York University Press, New York: 44–64.

Corner, J. (2010) "Politicality" and the inter-generic settings of reality television. In: Baruh, L. and Park, J. (eds.) *Reel Politics: Reality Television as a Platform for Political Discourse.* Cambridge Scholars Publishing, Newcastle upon Tyne: 22–39.

Couldry, N. (2003) *Media Rituals: a Critical Approach.* Routledge, London.

Couldry, N. (2004) Teaching us to fake it: The ritualized norms of television's "reality" games. In Murray, S. and Ouellette, L. (eds.) *Reality TV: Remaking Television Culture.* New York University Press, New York: 57–74.

Couldry, N. (2008) Reality TV or the secret theatre of neoliberalism. *Review of Education, Pedagogy, and Cultural Studies*, 30(1): 3–13.

Couldry, N. (2011a) Making populations appear. In: Kraidy, M. and Sender, K. (eds.) *The Politics of Reality Television: Global Perspectives.* Routledge, New York: 194–206.

Couldry, N. (2011b) Class and contemporary forms of "reality" production or, hidden injuries of class 2. In: Wood, H. and Skeggs, B. (eds.) *Reality Television and Class.* Palgrave Macmillan, New York: 33–44.

Crockett, R., Pruzinsky, T. and Persing, J. (2007) The influence of plastic surgery

References

"reality TV" on cosmetic surgery patient expectations and decisions making. *Plastic and Reconstructive Surgery*, 120(1): 316–24.

Crompton, R. (2008) *Class and Stratification*. Polity, Cambridge.

Dauncey, H. (2010) Regulation of television in France: Reality programming and the defense of French values. In: Baruh, L. and Park, J. (eds.) *Reel Politics: Reality Television as a Platform for Political Discourse*. Cambridge Scholars Publishing, Newcastle upon Tyne: 302–20.

David, A. (ed.) (2010) *Reality Matters: 19 Writers Come Clean About the Shows We Can't Stop Watching*. HarperCollins, New York.

Davis, K. (2003) *Dubious Equalities and Embodied Differences: Cultural Studies on Cosmetic Surgery*. Rowman & Littlefield, New York.

Deery, J. (2003) TV.com: Participatory viewing on the web. *Journal of Popular Culture*, 37(2): 161–83.

Deery, J. (2004a) Reality TV as advertisment. *Popular Communication*, 2(1): 1–19.

Deery, J. (2004b) Trading faces: The makeover show as prime-time infomercial. *Feminist Media Studies*, 4(2): 211–14.

Deery, J. (2006) Interior design: Commodifying self and place in the Extreme Makeover, Extreme Makeover: Home Edition, and The Swan. In: Heller, D. (ed.) *The Great American Makeover: Television, History, Nation*. Palgrave Macmillan, New York: 159–74.

Deery, J. (2012) *Consuming Reality: The Commercialization of Factual Entertainment*. Palgrave Macmillan, New York.

Deery, J. (2014) Mapping commercialization in reality television. In: Ouellette, L. (ed.) *A Companion to Reality Television*. Wiley Blackwell, Chichester: 11–28.

de Lesseps, L. (2009) *Class with the Countess*. Gotham, New York.

Devine, F., Savage, M., Scott, J. and Crompton, R. (eds.) (2005) *Rethinking Class: Culture, Identities and Lifestyle*. Palgrave Macmillan, New York

DiMattia, J. (2007) The gentle art of manscaping: Lessons in hetero-masculinity from the Queer Eye guys. In: Heller, D. (ed.) *Makeover Television: Realities Remodelled*. I.B. Tauris, New York: 133–49.

Dovey, J. (2000) *Freakshow: First Person Media and Factual Television*. Pluto, London.

Drew, E. (2011) Pretending to be postracial: The spectacularization of race in reality TV's Survivor. *Television & New Media*, 12(4): 326–46.

Dubrofsky, R. (2014) The Bachelorette's postfeminist therapy: Transforming women for love. In: Ouellette, L. (ed.) *A Companion to Reality Television*. Wiley Blackwell, Chichester: 191–207.

Dyer, R. (1986) *Heavenly Bodies: Film Stars and Society*. St. Martin's Press, New York.

Edwards, L. (2013) *The Triumph of Reality TV*. Praeger, Santa Barbara, CA.

Ellis, J. (2005) Documentary and truth on television: The crisis of 1999. In:

References

Corner, J. and Rosenthal, A. (eds.) *New Challenges for Documentary.* Manchester University Press, Manchester: 342–60.

Ewen, S. (1988) *All Consuming Images: The Politics of Style in Contemporary Culture.* Basic Books, New York.

Fetveit, A. (1999) Reality TV in the digital era: A paradox in visual culture? *Media Culture & Society,* 21(6): 787–804.

Fishman, M. (1998) Ratings and reality: the persistence of the reality crime genre. In: Fishman, M. and Cavender, G. (eds.) *Entertaining Crime: Television Reality Programs.* Walter de Gruyter, New York: 59–75.

Foucault, M. (1977 [1975]) *Discipline and Punish: the Birth of the Prison.* Pantheon, New York.

Fraser, K. (2007) "Now I am ready to tell how bodies are changed into different bodies ..." Ovid. In: Heller, D. (ed.) *Makeover Television: Realities Remodelled.* I.B. Tauris, New York: 177–92.

Gailey, E. (2007) Self-made women: Cosmetic surgery shows and the construction of female psychopathology. In: Heller, D. (ed.) *Makeover Television: Realities Remodelled.* I.B. Tauris, New York: 107–18.

Gamson, J. (1994) *Claims to Fame: Celebrity in Contemporary America.* University of California, Berkeley, CA.

Gamson, J. (2014) "It's been a while since I've seen, like, straight people": Queer visibility in the age of postnetwork reality television. In: Ouellette, L. (ed.) *A Companion to Reality Television.* Wiley Blackwell, Chichester: 227–46.

Giddens, A. (1991) *Modernity and Self-Identity: Self and Society in the Late Modern Age.* Stanford University Press, Stanford, CA.

Gill, R. (2007) *Gender and the Media.* Polity, Cambridge.

Gillan, J. (2011) *Television and New Media: Must-Click TV.* Routledge, New York.

Glynn, K. (2000) *Tabloid Culture: Trash Taste, Popular Power, and the Transformation of American Television.* Duke University Press, Durham, NC.

Godlewski, L. and Perse, E. (2010) Audience activity and reality television: Identification, online activity and satisfaction. *Communication Quarterly,* 58(2): 148–69.

Goffman, E. (1959) *The Presentation of Self in Everyday Life.* Anchor, New York.

Gray, H. (1995) *Watching Race: Television and the Struggle for "Blackness".* University of Minnesota Press, Minneapolis, MN.

Gray, J. (2009) Cinderella burps: Gender, performativity, and the dating show. In: Murray, S. and Ouellette, L. (eds.) *Reality TV: Remaking Television Culture,* 2nd edn. New York University Press, New York: 260–77.

Grindstaff, L. (2002) *The Money Shot: Trash, Class, and the Making of TV Talk Shows.* University of Chicago Press, Chicago, IL.

Grindstaff, L. (2011a) Just be yourself – only more so: Ordinary celebrity in the era of self-service television. In: Kraidy, M. and Sender, K. (eds.) *The Politics of Reality Television: Global Perspectives*. Routledge, New York: 44–57.

Grindstaff, L. (2011b) From Jerry Springer to Jersey Shore: The cultural politics of class in/on US reality programming. In: Wood, H. and Skeggs, B. (eds.) *Reality Television and Class*. Palgrave Macmillan, New York: 197–209.

Grindstaff, L. (2014) DI(t)Y, reality-style: The cultural work of ordinary celebrity. In: Ouellette, L. (ed.) *A Companion to Reality Television*. Wiley Blackwell, Chichester: 324–44.

Hardy, F. (ed.) (1966) *Grierson on Documentary*. Faber & Faber, London.

Harvey, D. (2007) *A Brief History of Neoliberalism*. Oxford University Press, New York.

Hasinoff, A. (2008) Fashioning race for the free market on America's Next Top Model. *Critical Studies in Media Communication*, 25(3): 324–43.

Hay, J. (2011) Extreme makeover: Iraq edition – "TV freedom" and other experiments for "advancing" liberal government in Iraq. In: Kackman, M., Binfield, M., Payne, M.T., Perlman, A. and Sebok, B. (eds.) *Flow TV: Television in the Age of Media Convergence*. Routledge, New York: 217–41.

Hearn, A. (2008) Insecure: Narratives and economies of the branded self in transformation television. *Continuum*, 22(4): 459–504.

Hearn, A. (2009) Hoaxing the "real": On the metanarrative of reality television. In: Murray, S. and Ouellette, L. (eds.) *Reality TV: Remaking Television Culture*, 2nd edn. New York University Press, New York: 165–78.

Hearn, A. (2010) Lightening in a bottle: Reality television, The Hills, and the limits of the immaterial labor thesis. In: Baruh, L. and Park, J. (eds.) *Reel Politics: Reality Television as a Platform for Political Discourse*. Cambridge Scholars Publishing, Newcastle upon Tyne: 232–48.

Heller, D. (2014) Wrecked: Programming celesbian reality. In: Weber, B. (ed.) *Reality Gendervision: Sexuality & Gender on Transatlantic Reality Television*. Duke University Press, Durham, NC: 123–46.

Hendershot, H. (2009) Belabored reality: making it work on The Simple Life and Project Runway. In: Murray, S. and Ouellette, L. (eds.) *Reality TV: Remaking Television Culture*, 2nd edn. New York University Press, New York: 243–59.

Hill, A. (2005) *Reality TV: Audiences and Popular Factual Television*. Routledge, London.

Hill, A. (2007) *Restyling Factual TV: Audiences and News, Documentary and Reality Genres*. Routledge, New York.

Hochschild, A. (1983) *The Managed Heart: Commercialization of Human Feeling*. University of California Press, Berkeley, CA.

Hollows, J. and Jones, S. (2010) "At least he's doing something": Moral entrepreneurship and individual responsibility in Jamie's Ministry of Food. *European Journal of Cultural Studies*, 13(3): 307–22.

Holmes, S. (2004a) "All you've got to worry about is the task, having a cup of tea, and doing a bit of sunbathing": Approaching celebrity in Big Brother. In:

References

Holmes, S. and Jermyn, D. (eds.) *Understanding Reality Television*. Routledge, New York: 111–35.

Holmes, S. (2004b) "But this time you choose!": Approaching the "interactive" audience in reality TV. *International Journal of Cultural Studies*, 3(2): 213–31.

Holmes, S. (2008) "Riveting and real – a family in the raw": (Re)visiting The Family (1974) after reality TV. *International Journal of Cultural Studies*, 11(2), 193–210.

Holmes, S. and Jermyn, D. (eds.) (2004) *Understanding Reality Television*. Routledge, New York.

Holmes, S. and Jermyn, D. (2014) The "pig", the "older women", and the "catfight": Gender, celebrity, and controversy in a decade of British reality TV. In: Weber, B. (ed.) *Reality Gendervision: Sexuality & Gender on Transatlantic Reality Television*. Duke University Press, Durham, NC: 37–53.

hooks, bell (2000) *Where We Stand: Class Matters*. Routledge, New York.

Jacobson, M. and Mazur, L. (1995) *Marketing Madness: A Survival Guide for a Consumer Society*. Westview Press, Boulder, CO.

Jenkins, H. (2006) *Convergence Culture: Where Old and New Media Collide*. New York University Press, New York.

Jermyn, D. (2004) "This is about real people!": Video technologies, actuality and affect in the television crime appeal. In: Holmes, S. and Jermyn, D. (eds.) *Understanding Reality Television*. Routledge, New York: 71–90.

Jhally, S. (1990) *The Codes of Advertising: Fetishism and the Political Economy of Meaning in the Consumer Society*. Routledge, New York.

Jones, J. (2003) Show your real face. *New Media & Society*, 5(3): 400–21.

Jones, M. (2008) *Skintight: An Anatomy of Cosmetic Surgery*. Berg, New York.

Jones, O. (2011) *Chavs: the Demonization of the Working Class*. Verso, London.

Jost, F. (2011) When reality TV is a job. In: Kraidy, M. and Sender, K. (eds.) *The Politics of Reality Television: Global Perspectives*. Routledge, New York: 31–43.

Kavka, M. (2008) *Reality Television, Affect and Intimacy: Reality Matters*. Palgrave Macmillan, New York.

Kavka, M. (2012) *Reality TV*. Edinburgh University Press, Edinburgh.

Kavka, M. (2014a) Reality TV and the gendered politics of flaunting. In: Weber, B. (ed.) *Reality Gendervision: Sexuality & Gender on Transatlantic Reality Television*. Duke University Press, Durham, NC: 54–75.

Kavka, M. (2014b) A matter of feeling: Mediated affect in reality television. In: Ouellette, L. (ed.) *A Companion to Reality Television*. Wiley Blackwell, Chichester: 459–77.

Kavka, M. and West, A. (2004) Temporalities of the real: Conceptualizing time in reality TV. In: Holmes, S. and Jermyn, D. (eds.) *Understanding Reality Television*. Routledge, New York: 136–53.

Kendall, D. (2011) *Framing Class: Media Representations of Wealth and Poverty in America*, 2nd edn. Rowman & Littlefield, Lanham, MD.

References

Klein, A. (2014) Abject femininity and compulsory masculinity on Jersey Shore. In: Weber, B. (ed.) *Reality Gendervision: Sexuality & Gender on Transatlantic Reality Television.* Duke University Press, Durham, NC: 149–69.

Kompare, D. (2004) Extraordinarily ordinary: The Osbournes as "An American Family." In: Murray, S. and Ouellette, L. (eds.) *Reality TV: Remaking Television Culture.* New York University Press, New York: 97–116.

Kraidy, M. (2010) *Reality TV and Arab Politics.* Cambridge University Press, Cambridge.

Kraidy, M. (2011) Reality television in new worlds. In: Kraidy, M. and Sender, K. (eds.) *The Politics of Reality Television: Global Perspectives.* Routledge, New York: 207–18.

Kraidy, M. and Sender, K. (eds.) (2011) *The Politics of Reality Television: Global Perspectives.* Routledge, New York.

Kraszewski, J. (2004) Country hicks and urban cliques: Mediating race, reality, and liberalism on MTV's The Real World. In: Murray, S. and Ouellette, L. (eds.) *Reality TV: Remaking Television Culture.* New York University Press, New York: 179–98.

Leggott, J. and Hochscherf, T. (2010) From the kitchen to 10 Downing Street: Jamie's School Dinners and the politics of reality cooking. In: Taddeo, J.A. and Dvorak, K. (eds.) *The Tube has Spoken: Reality TV and History.* Kentucky University Press, Lexington, KY: 47–64.

Lewis, T. (2008) *Smart Living: Lifestyle Media and Popular Expertise.* Peter Lang, New York.

Lewis, T. (2011) Globalizing lifestyles? Makeover television in Singapore. In: Kraidy, M. and Sender, K. (eds.) *The Politics of Reality Television: Global Perspectives.* Routledge, New York: 78–92.

Lewis, T. (2014) Life coaches, style mavens, and design gurus: Everyday experts on reality television. In: Ouellette, L. (ed.) *A Companion to Reality Television.* Wiley Blackwell, Chichester: 402–20.

Littleton, C. (2004) Burnett Interview. *Hollywood Reporter*, May 26. Available from: http://survivorskills.com/forum/index.php?topic=689.0;wap2

Luo, W. (2010) Chinese reality TV and politics: Entertainment vs. sociopolitical responsibility. In: Baruh, L. and Park, J. (eds.) *Reel Politics: Reality Television as a Platform for Political Discourse.* Cambridge Scholars Publishing, Newcastle upon Tyne: 165–81.

Magder, T. (2009) Television 2.0: The business of American television in transition. In: Murray, S. and Ouellette, L. (eds.) *Reality TV: Remaking Television Culture*, 2nd edn. New York University Press, New York: 141–64.

Malik, S. (2012) The Indian family on UK reality television: Convivial culture in salient contexts. *Television & New Media*, 14(6): 510–28.

Markey, C. and Markey, P. (2010) A correlational and experimental examination of reality television viewing and interest in cosmetic surgery. *Body Image*, 7(2): 165–71.

References

Marshall, P.D. (1997) *Celebrity and Power: Fame in Contemporary Culture.* University of Minnesota Press, Minneapolis, MN.

Mathijs, E. and Jones, J. (eds.) (2004) *Big Brother International: Formats, Critics and Publics.* Wallflower Press, London.

Mauss, M. (1990 [1950]) *The Gift: The Form and Reason for Exchange in Archaic Societies* (trans. W.D. Halls). Norton, New York.

Mayer, V. (2011a) *Below the Line: Producers and Production Studies in the New Television Economy.* Duke University Press, Durham, NC.

Mayer, V. (2011b) Reality television's "classrooms": Knowing, showing and telling about social class in reality casting and the college classroom. In: Wood, H. and Skeggs, B. (eds.) *Reality Television and Class.* Palgrave Macmillan, New York: 185–96.

Mayer, V. (2014) Cast-aways: The plights and pleasures of reality casting and production studies. In: Ouellette, L. (ed.) *A Companion to Reality Television.* Wiley Blackwell, Chichester: 57–73.

McAllister, M. (1996) *The Commercialization of American Culture: New Advertising, Control and Democracy.* Sage, Thousand Oaks, CA.

McCarthy, A. (2004) Stanley Milgram, Allen Funt, and me. In: Murray, S. and Ouellette, L. (eds.) *Reality TV: Remaking Television Culture.* New York University Press, New York: 19–39.

McCarthy, A. (2007) Reality television: A neoliberal theater of suffering. *Social Text,* 25(4): 17–42.

McMurria, J. (2009) Global realities: International markets, geopolitics, and the transcultural contexts of reality TV. In: Murray, S. and Ouellette, L. (eds.) *Reality TV: Remaking Television Culture,* 2nd edn. New York University Press, New York: 179–202.

McNair, A. (2010) Them boys are comin' for you: Black audience responses to Cops. In: Baruh, L. and Park, J. (eds.) *Reel Politics: Reality Television as a Platform for Political Discourse.* Cambridge Scholars Publishing, Newcastle upon Tyne: 115–33.

McRobbie, A. (2004) Notes on What Not to Wear and post-feminist symbolic violence. *The Sociological Review,* 52(2): 97–109.

Meltzer, K. (2010) A different sort of reality TV hero: Extreme fishermen, loggers, and truckers on the edge. In: Baruh, L. and Park, J. (eds.) *Reel Politics: Reality Television as a Platform for Political Discourse.* Cambridge Scholars Publishing, Newcastle upon Tyne: 249–64.

Miller, T. (2006) Metrosexuality: See the bright light of commodification shine! Watch yanqui masculinity made over! In: Heller, D. (ed.) *The Great American Makeover: Television, History, Nation.* Palgrave Macmillan, New York: 105–22.

Moran, A. (2014) Program format franchising in the age of reality television. In: Ouellette, L. (ed.) *A Companion to Reality Television.* Wiley Blackwell, Chichester: 74–93.

References

Morgan, K. (2009) Women and the knife: Cosmetic surgery and the colonization of women's bodies. In: Heyes, C. and Jones, M. (eds.) *Cosmetic Surgery: A Feminist Primer*. Ashgate, Burlington, VT: 49–77.

Moseley, R. (2000) Makeover takeover on British television. *Screen*, 41(3): 299–314.

Nabi, R. (2009) Cosmetic surgery makeover programs and intentions to undergo cosmetic enhancements: A consideration of three models of media effects. *Human Communication Research*, 35(1): 1–27.

Negra, D. (2013) Gender bifurcation in the recession economy: Extreme Couponing and Gold Rush Alaska. *Cinema Journal*, 53(1): 123–9.

Neiger, M. (2012) Cultural oxymora: The Israeli Idol negotiates meanings and readings. *Television & New Media*, 13(6): 535–50.

Nunn, H. (2011) Investing in the forever home: From property programming to "retreat TV." In: Wood, H. and Skeggs, B. (eds.) *Reality Television and Class*. Palgrave Macmillan, New York: 169–82.

Nunn, H. and Biressi, A. (2014) "Walking in another's shoes": Sentimentality and philanthropy on reality television. In: Ouellette, L. (ed.) *A Companion to Reality Television*. Wiley Blackwell, Chichester: 478–97.

Orbe, M., Warren, K. and Cornwell, N. (2001) Negotiating social stereotypes: Analyzing the Real World discourse by and about African American men. *International and Intercultural Communication Annual*, XXIII: 107–34.

Ouellette, L. (2004) "Take responsibility for yourself": Judge Judy and the neoliberal citizen. In: Murray, S. and Ouellette, L. (eds.) *Reality TV: Remaking Television Culture*. New York University Press, New York: 231–50.

Ouellette, L. (2014a) "It's not TV, it's birth control": Reality TV and the "problem" of teenage pregnancy. In: Weber, B. (ed.) *Reality Gendervision: Sexuality & Gender on Transatlantic Reality Television*. Duke University Press, Durham, NC: 236–58.

Ouellette, L. (ed.) (2014b) *A Companion to Reality Television*. Wiley Blackwell, Chichester.

Ouellette, L. and Hay, J. (2008) *Better Living Through Reality TV: Television and Post-Welfare Citizenship*. Blackwell, Oxford.

Pakulski, J. and Waters, M. (1996) *The Death of Class*. Sage, London.

Palmer, G. (2003) *Discipline and Liberty: Television and Governance*. Manchester University Press, Manchester.

Palmer, G. (2004) "The new you": Class and transformation in lifestyle television. In: Holmes, S. and Jermyn, D. (eds.) *Understanding Reality Television*. Routledge, New York: 173–90.

Palmer, G. (2011) Governing bodies. In: Kraidy, M. and Sender, K. (eds.) *The Politics of Reality Television: Global Perspectives*. Routledge, New York: 65–77.

Palmer, G. (2014) The wild bunch: Men, labor, and reality television. In:

References

Ouellette, L. (ed.) *A Companion to Reality Television*. Wiley Blackwell, Chichester: 247–63.

Papacharissi, Z. and Mendelson, A. (2007) An exploratory study of reality appeal. *Journal of Broadcasting and Electronic Media*, 51(2): 355–70.

Piper, H. (2004) Reality TV, Wife Swap and the drama of banality. *Screen*, 45(4): 273–86.

Poniewozik, J. (2008) Reality TV's working class heroes. *Time*, 22 May.

Poniewozik, J. (2012) Foreword. In: Wyatt, W. and Bunton, K. (eds.) *The Ethics of Reality TV: A Philosophical Examination*. Continuum: New York: ix–xi.

Pozner, J. (2010) *Reality Bites Back: The Troubling Truth about Guilty Pleasure TV*. Seal Press, Berkeley, CA.

Pramaggiore, M. and Negra, D. (2014) Keeping up with the aspirations: Commercial family values and the Kardashian brand. In: Weber, B. (ed.) *Reality Gendervision: Sexuality & Gender on Transatlantic Reality Television*. Duke University Press, Durham, NC: 76–96.

Pullen, C. (2004) The household, the basement and The Real World: Gay identity in the constructed reality environment. In: Holmes, S. and Jermyn, D. (eds.) *Understanding Reality Television*. Routledge, New York: 211–32.

Punathambekar, A. (2011) Reality television and the making of mobile publics: The case of Indian Idol. In: Kraidy, M. and Sender, K. (eds.) *The Politics of Reality Television: Global Perspectives*. Routledge, New York: 140–53.

Raphael, C. (2004) The political economic origins of reali-TV. In: Murray, S. and Ouellette, L. (eds.) *Reality TV: Remaking Television Culture*. New York University Press, New York: 119–36.

Redden, G. (2009) Economy and reflexivity in makeover television. In: Lewis, T. (ed.) *TV Transformations: Revealing the Makeover Show*. Routledge, New York: 45–54.

Ringrose, J. and Walkerdine, V. (2008) Regulating the abject: the TV make-over as site of neoliberal reinvention toward bourgeois femininity. *Feminist Media Studies*, 8(3): 227–45.

Robins, K. (1996) *Into the Image: Culture and Politics in the Field of Vision*. Routledge, London.

Rojek, C. (2001) *Celebrity*. Reaktion Books, London.

Roscoe, J. (2004) Watching Big Brother at work: A production study of Big Brother Australia. In: Mathijs, E. and Jones, J. (eds.) *Big Brother International: Formats, Critics and Publics*. Wallflower Press, London: 181–93.

Rose, N. (1996) *Inventing Our Selves: Psychology, Power, and Personhood*. Cambridge University Press, Cambridge.

Ross, A. (2014) Reality television and the political economy of amateurism. In: Ouellette, L. (ed.) *A Companion to Reality Television*. Wiley Blackwell, Chichester: 29–39.

Ross, S. (2008) *Beyond the Box: Television and the Internet*. Blackwell, Malden, MA.

References

Ruddock, A. (2010) "I'd rather be a cat than a poodle": What do celebrity politicians say about political communication? In: Baruh, L. and Park, J. (eds.) *Reel Politics: Reality Television as a Platform for Political Discourse*. Cambridge Scholars Publishing, Newcastle upon Tyne: 74–94.

Sager, M. (2001) What I've learned, Mark Burnett. *Esquire*, 136, July.

Sayer, A. (2005) *The Moral Significance of Class*. Cambridge University Press, Cambridge.

Sender, K. (2006) Queens for a day: Queer Eye for the Straight Guy and the neoliberal project. *Critical Studies in Media Communication*, 23(2): 131–51.

Sender, K. (2012) *The Makeover: Reality Television and Reflexive Audiences*. New York University Press, New York.

Sennett, R. (1992 [1974]) *The Fall of Public Man*. Norton, New York.

Shohat, E. and Stam, R. (1994) *Unthinking Eurocentrism*. Routledge, London.

Skeggs, B. (2004) *Class, Self, Culture*. Routledge, London.

Skeggs, B. (2005) The making of class through visualising moral subject formation. *Sociology*, 39(5): 965–82.

Skeggs, B. and Wood, H. (2009) The labor of transformation and circuits of value "around" reality television. In: Lewis, T. (ed.) *TV Transformations: Revealing the Makeover Show*. Routledge, New York: 119–32.

Skeggs, B. and Wood, H. (2012) *Reacting to Reality Television: Performance, Audience and Value*. Routledge, New York.

Smith, D. (2008) Critiquing reality-based televisual black fatherhood: A critical analysis of *Run's House* and *Snoop Dogg's Father Hood*. *Critical Studies in Media Communication*, 25(4): 393–412.

Smythe, D. (1981) *Dependency Road: Communications, Capitalism, Consciousness, and Canada*. Ablex, Norwood, NJ.

Springer, K. (2014) Jade Goody's preemptive hagiography: Neoliberal citizenship and reality TV celebrity. In: Weber, B. (ed.) *Reality Gendervision: Sexuality & Gender on Transatlantic Reality Television*. Duke University Press, Durham, NC: 211–31.

Squires, C. (2014) The conundrum of race and reality television. In: Ouellette, L. (ed.) *A Companion to Reality Television*. Wiley Blackwell, Chichester: 264–82.

Sun, W. and Zhao, Y. (2009) Television culture with "Chinese characteristics": the politics of compassion and education. In: Turner, G. and Tay, J. (eds.) *Understanding Television in the Post-Broadcast Era*. Routledge, London: 96–104.

Tait, S. (2007) Television and the domestication of cosmetic surgery. *Feminist Media Studies*, 7(20): 119–35.

Tasker, Y. and Negra, D. (eds.) (2007) *Interrogating Postfeminism: Gender and the Politics of Popular Culture*. Duke University Press, Durham, NC.

Thomas, L. (2008) "Ecoreality": The politics and aesthetics of "green" television.

References

In: Palmer, G. (ed.) *Exposing Lifestyle Television: The Big Reveal*. Ashgate, Burlington, VT: 177–88.

Tiggemann, M. (2005) Television and adolescent body image: The role of program content and viewing. *Journal of Social and Clinical Psychology*, 24: 361–81.

Tincknell, E. and Raghuram, P. (2002) Big Brother: Reconfiguring the "active" audience of cultural studies? *European Journal of Cultural Studies*, 5(2): 199–215.

Tolson, A. (2011) "I'm common and my talking is quite abrupt" (Jade Goody): Language and class in Celebrity Big Brother. In: Wood, H. and Skeggs, B. (eds.) *Reality Television and Class*. Palgrave Macmillan, New York: 45–59.

Turner, G. (2010) *Ordinary People and the Media: the Demotic Turn*. Sage, London.

Turner, G. and Tay, J. (eds.) (2009) *Television Studies after TV: Understanding Television in the Post-broadcast Era*. Routledge, London.

Tyler, I. and Bennett, B. (2010) "Celebrity chav": Fame, femininity and social class. *European Journal of Cultural Studies*, 13(3): 375–93.

Volcic, Z. and Andrejevic, M. (2011) Commercial nationalism on Balkan reality TV. In: Kraidy, M. and Sender, K. (eds.) *The Politics of Reality Television: Global Perspectives*. Routledge, New York: 113–26.

Wang, G. (2010) A shot at half-exposure: Asian Americans in reality TV shows. *Television & New Media*, 11(5): 404–27.

Watts, A. (2009) Melancholy, merit, and merchandise: The postwar audience participation show. In: Murray, S. and Ouellette, L. (eds.) *Reality TV: Remaking Television Culture*, 2nd edn. New York University Press, New York: 301–20.

Weber, B. (2009) *Makeover TV: Selfhood, Citizenship, and Celebrity*. Duke University Press, Durham, NC.

Weber, B. (2014) Mapping the makeover maze: The contours and contradictions of makeover television. In: Ouellette, L. (ed.) *A Companion to Reality Television*. Wiley Blackwell, Chichester: 369–85.

Weber, L. (2010) *Understanding Race, Class, Gender, and Sexuality: A Conceptual Framework*, 2nd edn. Oxford University Press, Oxford.

White, M. (2014) House hunters, real estate television and everyday cosmopolitanism. In: Ouellette, L. (ed.) *A Companion to Reality Television*. Wiley Blackwell, Chichester: 386–401.

Williams, R. (2010) Jamie Oliver's school dinners shown to have improved academic results. *The Guardian*, March 29.

Wilson, P. (2004) Jamming Big Brother: Webcasting, audience intervention, and narrative activism. In: Murray, S. and Ouellette, L. (eds.) *Reality TV: Remaking Television Culture*. New York University Press, New York: 323–43.

Wood, H. and Skeggs, B. (eds.) (2011a) *Reality Television and Class*. Palgrave Macmillan, New York.

References

Wood, H. and Skeggs, B (2011b) Reacting to reality TV: The affective economy of an "extended social/public realm." In: Kraidy, M. and Sender, K. (eds.) *The Politics of Reality Television: Global Perspectives.* Routledge, New York: 93–106.

Wray, M. (2006) *Not Quite White: White Trash and the Boundaries of Whiteness.* Duke University Press, Durham, NC.

Wray, M. and Newitz, A. (eds.) (1996) *White Trash: Race and Class in America.* Routledge, New York.

Wright, C. (2006) *Tribal Warfare, Survivor and the Political Unconscious of Reality Television.* Lexington Books, Oxford.

Yang, L. (2014) Reality talent shows in China: Transnational format, affective engagement, and the Chinese dream. In: Ouellette, L. (ed.) *A Companion to Reality Television.* Wiley Blackwell, Chichester: 516–40.

Index

Index

Index

Index

Index

Index

Index

Index